Praise for Andrew Wilson and *If God, Th*

A brilliant writer.
Bishop Wallace Benn

Don't buy a single copy of this book! Buy several, then give away copies to friends or contacts who are wrestling with the really big questions about the meaning and purpose of life, and who are wondering whether God could provide the answers they need. Andrew Wilson manages to dig deeply while using a light touch. He has produced a real page-turner that will surely be a huge help to many who read it.
John Blanchard, author and apologist

I have been on the lookout for a new voice on the apologetics scene for some time. Someone who manages to bring the big questions we have and the answers we seek down to earth, away from the philosophers and back to where we really are. Just like Jesus did. I have found what I am looking for.

Put very simply, this is the best book on apologetics that has come from these shores for a decade. It will bring a smile to your face and present numerous eureka moments. And Andrew does it in this mad conversational style. Right . . . time to lie down with a damp towel around my head.
★★★★★ *Christianity Magazine*

Andrew's book courageously journeys through the big questions we all wrestle with, questions about meaning and purpose. Drawing on the sciences and the arts, with a healthy cocktail of amusing anecdotes, this insightful book is an invitation to explore, to disagree with and engage with a conversation about making sense of life.
Andy Frost, Director, Share Jesus International

A rather impressive young Christian.
Ruth Gledhill, The Times

A remarkably gifted writer and Bible teacher.
Wayne Grudem

Last week I had the privilege of sharing the message of Jesus with over 1,000 students in Queens University, Belfast; I wish I could have given each of them a copy of this book. In a world where most students feel they have evolved from Christianity, Andrew's honest, informative, practical and most helpful book tackles ten key questions for those seeking truth and guidance. *If God, Then What?* should be read, highlighted and debated by every university student.
Mitch, evangelist with Crown Jesus Ministries and author of Snatched from the Fire

Intelligent, witty and disarming, Andrew has delivered a fascinating and engaging account of how we might find answers to the biggest questions of life. Who are we? Where are we going? And how can I get in on the good life? This book is easy to read and hard to put down. It is powerful, compelling stuff.
David Stroud, Newfrontiers UK

Dazzlingly good . . . There are plenty of books out there offering reasons for Christian hope. But not many of them grab you, from beginning to end, like this one. The mixture of sharp and honest arguments, striking anecdotes (funny as well as sober) and sheer imagination makes this a treat to read as well as an education.
Joel Virgo, Church of Christ the King, Brighton

if GOD

THEN WHAT?

For Anna Melody Wilson,
the beautiful little Missy

ANDREW WILSON

if GOD

THEN WHAT?

WONDERING ALOUD ABOUT
TRUTH, ORIGINS & REDEMPTION

ivp

INTER-VARSITY PRESS
Norton Street, Nottingham NG7 3HR, England
Email: ivp@ivpbooks.com
Website: www.ivpbooks.com

First published 2012

British Library Cataloguing in Publication Data
A catalogue record for this book is available from the British Library.

ISBN: 978–1–84474–569–2

Set in Dante 12/15pt
Typeset in Great Britain by CRB Associates, Potterhanworth, Lincolnshire
Printed and bound in Great Britain by the MPG Books Group

*Inter-Varsity Press publishes Christian books that are true to the Bible and that
communicate the gospel, develop discipleship and strengthen the church for its
mission in the world.*

*Inter-Varsity Press is closely linked with the Universities and Colleges Christian
Fellowship, a student movement connecting Christian Unions in universities and
colleges throughout Great Britain, and a member movement of the International
Fellowship of Evangelical Students. Website: www.uccf.org.uk*

CONTENTS

Acknowledgments   9

Prologue: Yale without the tuxedos
Where are we going?   10

1. Me and the *mutaween*
   What kind of evidence is there for that?   15
2. A Hercule Poirot thing
   How do we know?   31
3. Galactic roulette
   How did we get here?   48
4. Mind over matter
   Why do you think?   63
5. White rain
   What is possible?   77

Interval: The ripping of Mr Pritchard
Where are we so far?   91

6. A hornet in the icing
   What's wrong with the world?   96
7. The redemption of London
   What's the solution?   113

8. The Dublin display case
   What happened on 9 April AD 30?   129
9. Repainting God
   So what?   146

ACKNOWLEDGMENTS

Thank you so much, everybody who read this book and made it better by their comments: Nick Chatrath, Professor Chris Done, Jez Field, Toby Flint, Andy Frost, Wendy Grisham, Hannah Guckenheim, Chris Hartingdon, Matthew Herkes, Alex Jeffery, Andy Johnson, Fliss Johnston, Amy Newnham, Ellie Smith, Dr Ray Whitby and Declan Wiffen. I am extremely grateful to John Blanchard, Ruth Dickinson, Mitch, Steve Morris, David Stroud and Joel Virgo for their encouraging comments. Thanks to the team at IVP – Eleanor, Emily, Kath and Mollie in particular – and to the incomparable Richard Herkes: creativity and commitment don't always go together, but they do in your case. Kudos to Chris Mason for introducing me to Don Miller, and to Phil Moore for kicking the ball into your opponent's half. And most of all, as ever, my thanks to Rachel, with whom almost all the travelling and thinking for this book was done. Zeke and Anna are so lucky to have you, and so am I.

PROLOGUE.
YALE WITHOUT THE TUXEDOS: WHERE ARE WE GOING?

I've only been in trouble with the law three times, and each time it has been in America. That's strange for two reasons: because I've spent less than six months there in my thirty-two years, and because none of the things I got in trouble for would have been a problem in any other country I've visited. In 2006, I was pulled over by a guy with a gun for driving at thirty miles per hour in the open countryside in Maryland. In 2009, I incurred the wrath of Homeland Security in Chicago for failing to tick a box on behalf of my nine-month-old son to affirm that he had not, despite appearances, been involved in persecutions associated with Nazi Germany and its allies. (While we're on the subject, who actually ticks 'yes'?) And in 2000, most bizarrely of all, four of us were stopped by armed officers, and ordered to leave the area at once, for driving a car while wearing tuxedos and bow ties in Harlem.

I absolutely love America. There's nowhere like it on earth: big spaces, big cars, big skies, big hearts. But I've often found it decidedly odd that it's fine to chat on a mobile phone while driving on an interstate, and fine to carry a deadly weapon with you, but that infants are guilty of involvement with the

Holocaust until proven innocent, and police officers appear out of thin air if you're deemed to be overdressed in their largest city. I mean, I know British people in uniform were once a major threat to the security of cities on the Eastern Seaboard, but most of them were wearing red coats, not tuxedos, and not many were lost in the region of 125th and Lexington in a white Honda Civic at 2am.

We had been taking part in a university debating competition at Yale, which is one of the only things twenty-one-year-olds ever wear tuxes for. Debating competitions are fascinating things: you and your team get given a topic, and irrespective of what you think about it, you have to make the best arguments you can, either in favour of it or against it. So someone at the front says, 'This house believes we should let Turkey join the EU', and within a few minutes you have to make the most convincing case possible that this is either staringly obvious, or utterly unthinkable, depending on which side you're on, and the team that makes the best arguments goes through to the next round. After several hours of that, it was late, so we left Yale, drove back down the I-95 towards New York, bungled the directions, stopped twice in the South Bronx at hotels, which (it quickly turned out) rented their rooms by the hour not the night, and crossed the river into Harlem, at which point we were flagged down for our absurd outfits, and the guy driving was asked the extraordinary question, 'What are you doing in Harlem, sir?' We looked at one another desperately, but it seemed there wasn't an obvious answer. We were promptly instructed to leave the neighbourhood by the quickest route.

★ ★ ★

I learned a lot on that trip, but more than anything I learned how easy it is to convince yourself you're right. In a debating tournament, from the moment you're told which side you're on, it becomes your all-consuming task to make your opinion sound watertight and the other person's sound crass. It doesn't really matter whether what you're saying is true; what matters is that you argue for it better than the other guys. So it's not a very good way of arriving at the truth. Nobody ever stops and says, 'You know what, that's a good point, and it's changed my mind', because if you do that, you lose. And this means that you can walk into a room feeling open-minded about something, and leave it an hour later convinced that everyone who disagrees with you is a complete moron.

The scary thing is, that happens in normal life as well. I've been in lots of conversations where it's felt like changing my mind is 'losing', and being closed-minded is 'winning'. In fact, the more important the issue, the more unlikely we are to consider we might be mistaken. When it comes to the biggest questions of all – truth, origins, redemption, meaning – our perspective, our reputation and our very sense of self can become entangled, and it can seem like adjusting what we think would amount to an admission that we are somehow rubbish people. Throw us into a 'debate', and we could be at Yale, just without the tuxedos.

That's why I like questions. People in 'debate' don't normally ask questions, unless they're those annoying rhetorical 'How can you say that?' sort of questions. But people in conversations ask questions all the time, because they're the way you establish what someone else believes, and for that matter what you believe. Questions make conversations two-way, interested, open-minded, creative; debate speeches make them closed. I probably ask more questions in three minutes of conversation with my wife than I did in three years of university debating competitions, and it's because I genuinely care what she thinks. Love asks.

Since that debating trip, I've tried to ask questions more and more. The next time I set foot in New York, six years after being turfed out of Harlem as an arrogant student, I was a Christian pastor, and the process of repeatedly talking to people about meaning and spirituality had shown me the power of wondering aloud and asking questions. It got me into deep and meaningfuls with complete strangers in coffee shops and on buses, and it taught me how other people see the world, even when they started by saying that the worst thing about planet earth is religious people (which, especially since 9/11, they often have). It landed me in a live radio conversation with a guy who had lost a child, and couldn't understand how people believed God could exist when that sort of thing happened. Most of all, it showed me what sorts of questions helped people process the world around them.

* * *

I've found there are ten questions which are particularly helpful to ask ourselves, if we're ever wondering about truth, origins and redemption. I've put some of these questions to (literally) thousands of people, and the basic ten form the structure of the book you're now reading.

The first two questions are about how we come to believe things: 'What kind of evidence is there for that?' is about fundamentalism, and 'How do we know?' is about the nature of knowledge. The next three raise the question of God in relation to what we know about the universe ('How did we get here?'), the emergence of human life ('Why do you think?'), and the limits of what can happen in the world ('What is possible?'). Then there are two chapters about suffering and the possibility of redemption: 'What's wrong with the world?' and 'What's the solution?' The book then closes by asking: 'What happened on 9 April AD 30?' and 'So what?', two questions that engage more specifically with religious beliefs. Taken together, they all ask the big, tenth, question: 'If God, then what?' If, as the vast majority of inhabitants of this planet have believed, there is some sort of deity out there, what might that mean? And how could we find out?

Of course, this book doesn't just give a list of questions. It also gives the ways that I've tried to consider, wrestle with and answer them, through a series of stories, thoughts, conversations and travelling experiences. I'm sure the very process of writing a book means that I'll communicate an awful lot of what I think about things, so I can't pretend it's just a list of conversation starters. But I hope that, even if you don't agree at the moment with the answers I hold, you'll enjoy thinking through the questions. At a time when lots of people have given up on truth as troublesome, or meaning as mindless, these might be the ten most important questions in the world.

1.
ME AND THE MUTAWEEN: WHAT KIND OF EVIDENCE IS THERE FOR THAT?

I have only been called a fundamentalist once, and I was fourteen.

It was in the Memorial Block of my school, one of those castle-like buildings that people built after the war to make schools look imposing, with a tower and turrets and everything. When you walked in each morning, even in summer, you felt the building scowling at you, either because you had forgotten something, or just because you were there.

At the very top of the central staircase, right next to the door to the tower that was mysteriously always locked, was a grey, perpetually dark classroom that was imaginatively called Room 26, in which boys were taught divinity (which is a fancy word for religious studies). Teaching boys divinity was obviously needed in my school; that year, the Memorial Block was splashed across the centre pages of the *Daily Mail* because there had been a huge drugs bust in the school, and a whole bunch of pupils had been expelled. Having said that, perhaps the senior staff could have benefited from the lessons as well, since I later read in *The Times* that they had been rumbled by the Office of Fair Trading for being part of a price-fixing cartel with fifty other schools. Anyway, it was in Room 26, during a divinity lesson, that I was called a fundamentalist.

The man who said it was called RevKev. RevKev was the chaplain at my school, and he was one of the nicest people I have ever come across. Most people, if they were dressed in a long black chaplain's gown and walked into a grey, dark classroom full of fourteen-year-olds, would find it hard not to resemble Professor Snape from *Harry Potter*, but somehow RevKev managed it while looking warm and friendly. I think it was something to do with his face, which was a perfect circle, with a generous smile and a rather red nose in the exact middle, as if someone had pressed a large ripe blackberry in between his cheeks. In fact, RevKev was so nice that he could cheerfully call you a fundamentalist in front of twenty classmates, and because of the way he said it, you would take it as a compliment.

Back then, not many fourteen-year-olds knew what a fundamentalist was. I don't think I did either. It was in the early 1990s, about ten years before the strike on the Twin Towers, and none of us had ever seen the terrible results of fundamentalism: burning buildings, hook-handed hate preachers, suicide bombers, and the rest. It was a bit like being called a Nazi in the early 1930s, before anyone knew quite how bad it was. So when RevKev said it, I didn't feel like he was having a go at me. *A fundamentalist*, I thought. *That's nice. Believing in the fundamentals of something is important.* From the looks on the faces of my classmates, I don't think any of them realized quite what the chaplain was saying either.

It came up because I was arguing that Christians were right and everybody else was wrong. This was a common habit for me at school, partly because I enjoyed arguing, and partly because I was convinced I was right. As far as I could see, the Bible was true, and the Bible said certain things about ethics and religion and morality, things that meant that everyone who didn't believe them was wrong, and almost certainly going to hell. Something pretty much like this was believed by almost everyone I respected, and it had also been confirmed by my religious experience up to that point. So when faced with people who did not share this perspective in a divinity class, it was mainly my job to tell them that they were wrong and that I was right.

It had not yet occurred to me that you could use exactly the same argument with reference to the Qur'an, or the Talmud, or the Book of Mormon, or the Declaration of Independence for that matter. I hadn't noticed that billions of people in the world had had religious experiences and assumed their sacred texts were true, and that because their sacred texts said certain things about ethics and religion and morality, everyone else was wrong. I hadn't studied enough history to see the problems, even wars, that thinking like this could cause. Nor had I considered the implication that I might be wrong: but if I was, how would I know?

None of these things had become part of my thought life yet. It was just me in Room 26, representing Christianity, pitched into battle against one guy who thought Christians were odd because they didn't have sex before marriage, and another who wasn't sure there was any evidence for the Christian God, and another whose Sri Lankan parents were not Christians but wanted him to fit in when he went to school in England so they gave him the middle name 'Jehovah' – no, I'm not joking – and seventeen other people who seemed to agree with everything people said unless it was me saying it. And at the front of the class was RevKev, who thought all religions were equal, and all of us were reaching for the same god, and the only people who were wrong were the ones who thought theirs was the only way.

So he called me a fundamentalist. And he was right.

★ ★ ★

A few minutes ago, I was watching a YouTube clip in which Derren Brown was talking about why he wasn't a believer in God. Derren Brown is a very clever television magician who presents his tricks as a mind-control act, and he was saying that he had stopped believing in God as a teenager because his pastors and others motivated people by fear, and were scared of investigating the evidence for their beliefs. The clip was only four minutes long, but it was plenty long enough to make me think that Derren Brown had probably met people like me when he was a teenager. Then I started thinking about all the people I knew at school, and I wondered how many of them could make a YouTube clip, explaining that they didn't believe in God because they had met fundamentalists like me, individuals who were scared of finding out whether or not their beliefs were true. It made me think.

★ ★ ★

It was several years before I realized what RevKev meant. For most of my life at school, belief in God was something to be defended if the subject came up in conversation, but otherwise a bit of a side issue. The main things at school were being popular, being good at sport, being thought funny, getting drunk in such a way that you were noticed by all of your friends and none of your teachers, and doing well at exams without being picked on for it. Since believing in God didn't help me with most of these, I didn't really think about it much. When religion did come up in conversation, I usually saw it as a battle which could either be won or lost, and because I was quite an articulate and aggressive person, I usually won. The idea that I ought to be debating rather than battling – or better still, discovering for myself whether what I believed was true or not – didn't really come up.

I think that's quite common amongst fundamentalists: the language of winning and losing. When we make our belief system part of our identity, and we start valuing ourselves by the accuracy of our ideas, then it's very easy for a statement like *this is true* to become *we are right*, and for that to turn into *we are winning*, and then *we are better*. Every debate won is another mini-victory in the global war taking place between our ideas and other people's, and it makes us feel better about ourselves, because our sense of worth is tied to our sense of rightness. (Mine was, anyway. I was a scrawny teenager with acne and no girlfriend, so doubtless being right was my way of getting credibility with other people, of feeling more worthwhile.) When we're young, we're incredibly vulnerable to this, because we are searching so desperately for affirmation; I'll bet this is part of the belief system of most young men who physically blow themselves up to help 'win' an ideological 'war'. I wonder if most of them have ever even considered that their views might be wrong, or asked themselves how they might find out. In this sort of war, admitting that you are wrong is the worst possible outcome, so you don't even think about it.

Last year I watched a Jamie Foxx film called *The Kingdom*, in which US agents were involved in a mission in Saudi Arabia, and the only thing I remember about it was the ending. There was an old woman, wrapped in a shawl and sitting on her steps, muttering with quiet menace about the Americans, in Arabic: *We're going to kill them all.* Then it cut to Jamie Foxx in Langley, Virginia, as he explained what he had said to another character earlier in the movie, about the Saudis: *I said, we're going to kill them all.* And I thought that was a very interesting comment about fundamentalism, because the filmmakers seemed to be saying that the American agents in the film were just as fundamentalist as the Saudi characters. Since the Iraq war, it has become fashionable to say things like this, but it's still true. Fundamentalism can happen within Islam, Christianity, liberal democracy and even secularism, because it happens when people refuse to question what they believe, based on evidence, and decide to pursue victory instead of discovery. I lived like that for years.

Having said that, I never blew anybody up at school. I never killed anyone, or hit anyone, for disagreeing with me. So it might sound a bit melodramatic to compare myself with Mohammed Atta, as if we were both basically struggling with the same sort of problem. But I still think RevKev was right about me. I heard a lecture at UC Berkeley that described the four phases of fundamentalism, in which the lecturer said it goes: superiority → isolation → caricature → persecution. If you think that you're right and others are wrong, then you're likely to look down on them. If you look down on them, you will often end up separating yourself from them, and that's where ghettos and gulags and gated communities come from. If you do that, you'll forget what other people are really like, and you'll caricature them. And if you caricature people for long enough, it won't be long before persecution starts. This is what happened with the Nazis, and apartheid, and the Wars of Religion, and suicide bombers, and I was well on the way by the age of fourteen. If I hadn't been in a school surrounded by people who disagreed with me, it could have been a lot worse.

Now I'm not a sociologist, and I don't want to be trivial about something so serious, but that lecture at UC Berkeley all sounds about right. And if it is, then Mohammed Atta and the Spanish Inquisition and Heinrich Himmler and I all had pretty much the same problem, in different degrees. How troubling.

* * *

You never forget the first place you see fundamentalism for yourself, and for me it was Kano.

Africa is an extraordinary continent, and Nigeria is about as African and extraordinary as it gets. The capital city, Abuja, didn't even exist a generation ago, and it sits, baffled, in the centre of a large, overpopulated and chaotic country, administering affairs with a mixture of desperation and eccentricity. To the south, the landscape is lush, green and tropical: colourfully dressed women line the main roads carrying baskets of fruit on their heads, the locals are almost entirely black African, and there are churches with convoluted names on every street corner, like 'The Unified Cherubim and Seraphim Students' Church'. As you drive north of Abuja, and particularly when you pass Kaduna, the country changes. Green gives way to brown, lush tropical vegetation becomes dusty scrubland, English turns into Arabic, black faces become brown, colourful outfits become white, and the churches are replaced by mosques. It's as if somebody drew a line somewhere in the middle of Nigeria and announced that it was the dividing line between northern and southern Africa. Maybe they did.

At the north of the country is Kano, a suffocatingly hot, sprawling and dusty city with an official population of 3 million, although the real figure may be three times that. We reached it after a hair-raising journey over potholed roads in a clapped-out minibus, at eighty miles per hour, in a thunderstorm, in the dark, while the driver talked on his mobile phone, so our first impression of Kano was that of a sleep-filled haven, safe from lightning bolts and crazy drivers. The following morning, however, we stepped out into what was then, and is still, the most unpleasant place I have ever seen. It began with the smell, which had something to do with the exhaust from a million motorbikes, and an awful lot to do with the open drainage system, which was no more than a set of roadside gutters along which sewage was drifting slowly. Then there was the rubbish, which was everywhere: not just crisp packets and Coke cans, but generous mountains of trash lining the streets, several feet high, rotting in the June sun and adding to the stench. It didn't make a great first impression.

Officially, the secular national government was in charge of the city, but Kano was a sharia state with a local emir, which meant in practice that the real power lay with the *mutaween*. These are the unofficial Islamic religious police, who enforce sharia law whenever they choose to. We spoke to several non-Muslims there who told us that healthcare and education were free only if they converted to Islam, which presented many families with a terrible choice. In some countries, the *mutaween* have gone further: in 2002, they banned young women from leaving a burning building in Mecca because they weren't dressed properly or accompanied by a man. Fifteen girls died. It's not as extreme as that in Kano yet, but when the *mutaween* decide that women cannot ride on motorbikes for religious reasons, whatever those are, the women have to stop instantly for fear of punishment. It's that simple. A quick decision, and half the city's population are suddenly deprived of the only affordable form of transport.

It was a tense place. When you drove around, you were occasionally stopped by men with guns: they were usually just the army, checking that you weren't bandits, but you couldn't be sure of that until they lifted the roadblock. We got an idea of how tense it was when we visited a church that had recently been burned to the ground by Islamists. We were there to document what had happened, and were quickly surrounded by a large crowd of angry young men, shouting at us in Hausa and insisting that we were not allowed in the area. I say crowd, but there's not much of a difference between a crowd and a mob, particularly when you're a white, English-speaking infidel, travelling with your petite, blonde, English-speaking infidel wife in a heavily Islamic area, and they're standing in a circle around you. Apparently, the problem was that we had not requested permission to be there, and certainly not to ask questions about what had happened, and that meant trouble. Thanks to some apologetic grovelling from our Nigerian guides – which, you would think, ought not to be necessary for standing in a public street in a free country looking at a public building – we escaped without harm, but there were times when I thought we wouldn't. Clearly, I thought, this was not a place where free enquiry was encouraged.

Now I think Kano fits very well with that lecture at UC Berkeley. In Nigeria, as in so many places, you can certainly see superiority leading to isolation, as Christians and Muslims separate themselves from people who don't share their religion. You can also see this isolation developing into caricature; almost every Christian we spoke to believed that Muslims were responsible for all problems, and vice versa. And predictably, you can see this caricature resulting in persecution, which explains the burned churches and mob violence, in this case from the majority Muslims to the minority Christians. It's tragic, when you think about it. All those people suffering, because people don't ask questions about what they believe.

But my lasting memory of Kano was not the burned churches, the rubbish, the open sewers, the heat, the tension or the *mutaween*. It was summed up in a photo I took of two boys, waiting on the side of a street. The backdrop was both everyday and apocalyptic at the same time, rather like Kano itself – an arid, dusty day, with scraggly and tumbledown accommodation stretching for miles in every direction, and rubbish being blown along in the hot wind. It was like something from T. S. Eliot's *The Waste Land*:

What are the roots that clutch, what branches grow
Out of this stony rubbish? Son of man,
You cannot say, or guess, for you know only
A heap of broken images, where the sun beats,
And the dead tree gives no shelter, the cricket no relief,
And the dry stone no sound of water . . .
I will show you fear in a handful of dust.

Behind the two boys was a whitewashed wall, and on it a piece of graffiti – chilling, ironic and comic all at once, given the lack of education, the oppression and the pollution all around it. Someone had scrawled a sentence in blood-red letters, and it illustrated perfectly the blind sense of superiority I was just talking about. It said: 'Sharia is the best way of life.'

I wasn't convinced.

★ ★ ★

Coming back from Kano, I wondered: how do you stop the slide? How do you stop teenage boys like me being arrogant and bigoted, and people in Kano imposing sharia or burning down churches? What am I supposed to say about those Christians who hold up signs in America saying, 'God hates fags', or about the Taliban, or about Saudi Arabia's treatment of women, or about Hindu extremists who burn Indian villages, or communist dictators who try to wipe out religious belief, or atheists on the internet who say that no amount of evidence could convince them that a supernatural event had happened? Is there anything I can do about that sort of unquestioning fundamentalism, or do I just have to lump it?

I've thought about that quite a lot since then.

★ ★ ★

My fundamentalism imploded at university. It's pretty hard to believe you're right and everyone else is wrong when you're surrounded by people who are much cleverer than you, and who ask you questions for which you have no answers. My friends used to sit around listening to Shostakovich and talking about Hegel and Derrida, and I came to realize that I didn't really know anything about anything. My friend Richard did a PhD in the concept of the self in Western Marxism, and went on to teach philosophy at the University of Chicago. My other friend James knew an astonishing amount about literature, art and music, and had written both a novel and a poetry anthology before he even started his degree. Then there was my flatmate Greg, who studied Anglo-American philosophy, had the fastest mind I've ever come across, and ended up winning a Fulbright Scholarship to Harvard. When these people debated things, I often just sat and listened, because it was so stimulating. I still remember one 3am debate about the flexibility of language, when James exclaimed, 'Words are life and death to me!' and, in a flash, Greg responded, 'But life and death are words to me.' They were quite awe-inspiring to be around, in that way.

But they made it almost impossible to be a fundamentalist. When I was talking to them, it became embarrassingly obvious that I didn't have very good reasons for believing what I believed, because they asked such awkward questions. What evidence was there that the Bible was divinely inspired? An all-loving, all-powerful God would stop pointless suffering, wouldn't he? Why should the opinions of a few religious oddballs from two thousand years ago have any influence at all in the modern world? Aren't miracles by definition imposs-ible, and therefore to be rejected? Put bluntly, is there any evidence whatsoever for the existence of the Christian God? And so on. While I reflected on questions like these, they moved on to discuss political theory, or whether art was dead, or whatever. And I sat there thinking, wondering whether there was any reason to believe in Christianity at all.

I don't know if you've ever been in a conversation like that, where everything you believe is being challenged by people who are cleverer than you, and you aren't sure whether you have a leg to stand on. If you have, you'll know that you have two options. One, you can investigate what you believe, to find out whether or not there is any evidence for it. Or two, you can decide not to investigate, because your beliefs are really a question of faith – they are your opinions and none of anybody else's business, and that's that. If you choose option one, you run the risk of finding out that you have been wrong for years, which most people don't like very much. But if you choose option two, you are doomed to be completely irrelevant, because what you believe has no evidence that other people can understand or critique.

Now, fundamentalists don't generally get into conversations like this in the first place, because we surround ourselves with people who agree with us. If we do, we generally choose option two, because we don't want to entertain the idea that we might be wrong. For some reason, though – maybe it was because I really liked my friends, or maybe I was just more worried about being irrelevant than being proved wrong – I chose option one.

The atheist Richard Dawkins and I disagree about quite a few things, but we do agree about one thing. He has written a book arguing that people like me are delusional, and I have argued against his ideas in print and on the radio, resulting in some pretty unpleasant comments about me and my book on his website. But we agree about fundamentalism. In *A Devil's Chaplain*, he says, 'Next time that somebody tells you that something is true, why not say to them: "What kind of evidence is there for that?" And if they can't give you a good answer, I hope you'll think very carefully before you believe a word they say.'

I think he's absolutely right. Faith without reason, the sort of belief without evidence that I had until I was about twenty, is bizarre.

* * *

This isn't a new idea, mind you. It's not as if the whole world was blundering on in darkness for thousands of years, until in the eighteenth century some white guys in Europe discovered evidence and announced to the rest of humanity that we needed to have reasons for what we believed. I know that sounds obvious, but to listen to some people these days, you'd think that's what had happened. In fact, lots of the ancients knew very well that beliefs needed to be grounded in evidence, and that this evidence needed to come in the form of public events, not private experiences.

That's why the Hebrew prophet Elijah set up a massive experiment on Mount Carmel, and said, 'The God who answers by fire – he is God.' That's why so many Greek philosophers had no time for popular religion that couldn't be demonstrated from evidence. That's why the apostle Paul did not kiss reason goodbye when he proclaimed the Christian message: 'If Christ has not been raised, then our preaching is useless and so is your faith.' These aren't the sorts of things that fundamentalists say. You only say these things if you are committed to answering the question: 'What kind of evidence is there for that?'

On the other side of the coin, lots of people today believe things without any evidence at all. Some people still believe that Elvis is alive, or that the earth is flat. I'm always surprised by how many people believe that you lose 70% of your body heat through your head – this must have been invented by a hat salesman somewhere, because if it were true, it would mean that you would be far warmer on a winter's day wearing a woolly hat and nothing else, than wearing normal clothes and no hat. A poll for *Die Zeit* in 2003 reported that 31% of Germans under thirty believed the US government was responsible for 9/11. And so on.

On a much wider scale, there are literally billions of people in the world today, including a lot of religious people, who don't have any evidence whatsoever for believing in their gods – and in fairness, they don't claim that they do. If you asked them what kind of evidence there was for belief in astrology, or Hinduism, or Kabbalah, or Sunni Islam, they would look at you as if you were a complete idiot (and if you don't believe me, try it). Oddly, quite a lot of secular people are the same – it's weird how many people say things like, 'Science has disproved God' (how would that work?), or 'Faith means believing things without any evidence', or 'Religions are the cause of all wars', not because there's any evidence for those things, but just because they've heard other people say them. I'm not sure fundamentalism is limited to religious people.

Three years ago, for instance, I was reading a book called *The God Delusion*, and I found a surprising number of mistakes in the bit where it talked about the Bible. I mean, lots of people like picking holes in the Bible, but the author, who was an Oxford professor, didn't seem to know anything about it. He thought that Matthew and Luke disagreed about the virgin birth, and about Jesus being descended from David and born in Bethlehem. He thought Luke told the story of the three kings, and Matthew contradicted him. He thought Paul wrote Hebrews, and Bart Ehrman was at Princeton. And he said all sorts of other things that a quick flick through a New Testament, or a Google search, could have shown were untrue.

People make mistakes. Even Oxford professors make mistakes, although they don't usually make that many in such a short space of time. But here's the odd thing. When I pointed out these mistakes in debates with people, in print and on the radio, people often said simply that theology wasn't a real subject, and that you couldn't expect atheists to take it seriously, so who cares if they got their facts wrong about it? And I thought: but what if everybody said that? What if everybody thought, *I know I'm right, so the other view is wrong, so there can't be any evidence for it, so I don't need to bother checking.* Surely that is exactly what fundamentalists do? Isn't that the very thing that atheists are opposing?

I guess I'm saying that lots of people don't think evidence is particularly important. But I have to disagree. I mean, it doesn't really matter if people hold private opinions without evidence about things that don't affect anyone else, like the amount of heat that escapes from your head. But I don't think our most important beliefs work that way. I think all views of the world, whether they are religious or not, claim to be accounts of the whole of reality – good and evil, beauty and tragedy, right and wrong, life and death. We live in a world where people disagree about these things, and yet we need to find common ground so we can make laws and discuss global problems and solutions. This means public dialogue is extremely important. And that means we need evidence for what we believe.

* * *

So I used to be a fundamentalist, and now I'm not. I used to think that what I believed was true because I was brought up to believe it; now, I try not to accept anything unless there is good evidence for it. For some time, there was quite a lot of overlap between me and the *mutaween*, but these days I probably share more common ground with Richard Dawkins. It's been an odd journey, really.

2.
A HERCULE POIROT THING: HOW DO WE KNOW?

I don't know if you find this, but I frequently get muddled up between movies that I've seen. Lots of them are just so similar to each other. Watch a few Harrison Ford films, and it's hard to distinguish between each decent, hard-working family man who gets caught up in some miscarriage of justice or other, and then beats the bad guys in a disarmingly normal sort of way, almost certainly involving an American flag somewhere. When you've watched more than two submarine movies, you know that there's going to be a scene where the salty old seadog tells you what it's like to be attacked with depth charges, and then another scene when it happens just like he said and the camera pans significantly into his old, lined, grimacing face, and then another scene when water bursts into the cabin and everybody runs around, shouting. Or how about those identikit stories about brilliant-but-arrogant young hotshots who get mentored by wily and dis-illusioned old pros, frequently played by Gene Hackman, but end up coming good in the end? Is there a package somewhere that movie producers can buy, I wonder?

But one film that I've never got muddled up is *The Matrix*. I'd be willing to bet that nobody who's seen it has forgotten whether or not they have. And I don't think that's because of the story (which is rather silly), or the cast (which is fine, but makes Hugo Weaving such a cartoon that when you see him in *Lord of the Rings* you expect him to don black shades and say 'Mister Anderson' in a leering, sinister voice), or the style (which is iconic, but glorifies mass murder by setting it to knee-length black leather jackets and the Propellerheads). I think *The Matrix* is memorable because it takes one of the most important philosophical questions there is, asks it in a way that makes you want to know the answer, and leaves you scratching your head as you walk out the cinema. The question, in essence, is this: how do you know?

★ ★ ★

For those who haven't seen *The Matrix*, it is set somewhere around 2200, and intelligent robots have taken over the earth. Human beings are now trapped in pink capsules where their brain energy is being harvested by robots, yet they all believe they are living in a normal world, because the robots have uploaded a complex computer simulation, 'the Matrix', into their brains. In a central scene, Larry Fishburne explains all this to Keanu Reeves, and asks, 'How do you define real? If you're talking about what you can feel, what you can smell, what you can taste and see, then real is simply electrical signals interpreted by your brain. This is the world that you know . . . The Matrix is a computer-generated dream-world built to keep us under control.'

All of this is very entertaining, and very well played by Larry Fishburne (who, while we're on the subject of important questions, now has shoulders three times larger than they were in *Apocalypse Now*. What is that about?). But it is also rather unsettling, because you find yourself wondering: how do I know that the world around *me* is real, and that I am not being harvested by a robot in a capsule somewhere? Am I sitting in a cinema right now, or is it just that I believe I am, because a computer program is tricking me? And how would I know?

The people who made *The Matrix* were not the first to come up with this, of course. In 1641, René Descartes imagined an all-powerful demon was trying to deceive him, and tried to work out how he could know for certain that he was actually there. These days, philosophers talk more about how you know you're not a brain in a vat, which is another way of expressing the same problem. But I like the way they do it in *The Matrix*. It's not easy to get teenagers debating epistemology on their way home from the movies.

The thing is, although we all talked about it on our way out of the cinema, none of our immediate answers seemed to work. You might have gone with, 'because it's obvious' – but then it would be, wouldn't it? Or, 'because everybody agrees with me' – but they would, wouldn't they? Maybe you'd prefer, 'because I can see things with my eyes, and feel them with my hands' – but again, this would feel like it was true, even if you were in the Matrix, and there was no real world beyond. So there wasn't an easy answer.

I don't know if anyone who watched the movie got so paralysed by doubt that they stopped living life altogether, or tried to escape from the pink capsule they now believed was surrounding them. I doubt it. Most of us probably just got on with life, assuming there was a good answer out there somewhere. But I reckon the question will have lodged in a lot of people's minds for a while, and it will have bothered quite a few of us. How do we *know* we're really here? And if we don't know for sure that we're really here, then how do we know that $1 + 1 = 2$? Or that water boils? Or that God exists, or doesn't? How do we know anything?

* * *

Have you ever wondered if your dreams were the real world, and the real world was just a very vivid dream? When I was a kid, I sometimes used to pinch myself in normal life, to check that it wasn't a very long, very convincing dream. But what if the pinching was part of the dream? How would I find out?

* * *

Some would answer: you can't. I came across a fair bit of this at university: you can know about your sense experiences, but you can't know anything at all about what the 'real' world is actually like. This position is sometimes called *phenomenalism*, because it says we can know about the phenomena we experience, but not about any reality that they might point towards or be caused by. So I can't know that I am drinking a nice hot cup of coffee. I can only know that I experience the sensation of heat, wetness and coffee flavour when I open my mouth (if I have one) and put my lips to the cup (or is there even a cup?). It is simply impossible to know that there isn't a mad scientist, or futuristic robot, or malicious demon, making me think those things. Yikes.

Others would say: what a lot of cobblers. Of course I can know that I'm here – because if I'm not, then who is asking all these questions? It's incredibly obvious that we can know things about the world. And the way we know things is by proving them. This is sometimes called *positivism*: there are some things we can know about for sure, because we can check they are true, either by definition ($1 + 1 = 2$) or by scientific experiment (water boils). These are the sorts of things we can know. If something can't be known by maths or science – and, of course, the statement 'God exists' falls into this category – then it isn't something you can know, because you have no way of being sure whether it's true or not. Either knowledge is provable by scientific methods, or it isn't actually knowledge at all.

⋆ ⋆ ⋆

I doubt there are that many phenomenalists around these days, except in philosophy departments. It's all just a bit too weird to live that way. I mean, you might accept the idea in principle, but in practice you'll probably process the world exactly the same way as everyone else.

There are plenty of positivists, though. I can't remember the number of times someone has asked me why I believe in God when I can't prove he exists, as if I should be able to do a laboratory experiment or something. People who talk like this are usually positivists.

A few years ago, I met a guy called John who used to do schools work in Nottingham. He would go into assemblies and talk to hundreds of students about God, and then at the end he would take open questions. The first question was almost always this, shouted out aggressively: 'HAVE . . . YOU . . . SEEN . . . GOD?!' As he paused to consider his answer, John said he could see the students turn to one another in excitement, believing that they had trapped him. But John had a one-liner that he always used to give. 'I would have seen God,' he would say, 'if I had lived at the right time. Have you seen Queen Victoria?'

That would tend to quieten things for a while, as the student tried to answer in a way that didn't make him look silly in front of his friends. But apparently, question two was just as predictable. John said it was almost certain that the second person would say, 'All right then – you prove to me there's a god!' (This is a classic example of what I've been talking about: 'If what you're saying is true, then you ought to be able to prove it.') So John would then explain that not all knowledge was scientific or mathematic, and talk about how other sorts of human knowledge worked, including knowledge of God. To most students, it just wasn't something they had ever thought about.

I think people like this need to be asked the question: 'How do you know?' I think their problem is that they haven't noticed something really important: that *most of the things they believe cannot be proved by maths or by science*. Most of them believe there was a First World War, even though they can't do tests in a laboratory to prove it. Nobody can do a repeatable experiment on the statement: 'George Washington was president', or 'Charles Dickens wrote *A Christmas Carol*', let alone 'I love you' or 'Mozart is brilliant' or 'genocide is wrong', or even 'knowledge has to be provable'. So how do they know those things? I've often wondered about that.

Do you see what I mean? Most of the things I say in a day, and most of the things I know about the world, cannot be proven scientifically. It's not that scientific methods aren't important; it's just that they can't help us with a lot of human knowledge. Come to think of it, you can't even do a scientific experiment to prove that you are there now, reading this book. So I don't think positivism helps us with the demon, the vat, the dream, or the Matrix.

★ ★ ★

I was bamboozled by all this for quite a while. Part of me wanted to round up and shoot all philosophers for creating puzzles like this in the first place, preferring to let common sense do its thing. Part of me wanted to carry on living as if none of this was a problem. But another part of me wanted a decent answer, an explanation for how I know things – that I exist, that water boils and that George Washington was president. Maybe, I thought, if I could find a way of knowing that would fit all of these statements, I could apply that sort of method to God. And then I would know what I was looking for.

I'm a bit embarrassed to admit it, but I was rescued by two sentences in *The Oxford Companion to Philosophy*, which was one of the books I would flick through at university in an attempt to look clever. (This is silly, really, because if I genuinely knew about philosophy, then I wouldn't be reading the duffer's guide in some dictionary, and all my friends knew that.) Not many people would say their life was changed by reading a philosophy dictionary. But here's the quotation that cleared some of the fog, and helped disentangle me from the Matrix:

Do you know that you are looking at a . . . book right now rather than, say, having your brain intricately stimulated by a mad scientist? The sceptic carefully describes this alternative so that no experiment can refute it. The conclusion that you really are looking at a book, however, explains the aggregate of your experiences better than the mad scientist hypothesis or any other competing view.

It might not sound much, but I thought that was pretty profound. I can't do an experiment to prove that I'm sitting here, rather than being in the Matrix, or a dream, or a vat. But the explanation that I am sitting here 'explains the aggregate of [my] experiences better'. When I read that, I instantly felt rather stupid for not having thought of it before.

Let's put it this way. I am having certain experiences right now: the sounds of conversations and espresso machines and pounding raindrops and strong November winds buffeting outside, the aroma and flavour of a tall drip coffee, the feel of the rain in my hair slowly creeping down the back of my neck, the sights of tables and cups and books and small children. (I'm often astonished by how many parents feel the urge to take their crying toddlers to Starbucks whenever I decide to go and write there; when did you last see a child enjoying a cappuccino?) And there are two explanations for those experiences. I might be actually sitting in Starbucks, or I might be in the Matrix or a vat, with outside agents (like robots or scientists) making me experience those things.

Of course, I can't do a scientific experiment to prove which it is. But the Starbucks-explanation is a better explanation for the data than the Matrix-explanation. It is simpler, because it doesn't require a whole other world to be there, complete with intelligent robots, dreamworld software, pink capsules and Hugo Weaving. It includes all the evidence. And it is coherent, with no random piece of information that doesn't fit. It 'explains the aggregate of my experiences better'.

This realization made quite an impact on me. I remember reading and thinking about it on a train from Leicester to St Pancras, and trying to work out the implications. At Market Harborough, I was more concerned than anything else: *Most things I believe at the moment can't be proved. This is a problem.*

By Kettering, I was questioning: *Does that matter? What if knowledge isn't about finding iron-clad proof, but about finding the best explanation?*

And so it went on, through Wellingborough, Bedford, Luton, St Albans. *So, unless you're in a maths classroom, or maybe a lab, you'll never prove things for certain. But that's OK. You can still find the best explanation, and that's how we know things.*

By the time I reached St Pancras, I felt a lot better. So I bought a large traditional Cornish pasty from a street vendor, caught the next Tube to Highbury and Islington, and day-dreamed about the weekend.

* * *

I've come to think that this is true of big things, as well as little things. I used to think that I ought to be able to 'prove' what I believed about everything, as if it were possible to take someone logically through my entire worldview, step by step, so that only an idiot would disagree with what I was saying. But I tend not to talk like that now, mainly because I've realized that every system of belief has to start from somewhere, and the place you choose to start from affects your conclusion. So if I start from 'I think, therefore I am', I'll end up in a different place than if I start from 'In the beginning, God'. That's one reason why brilliant philosophers like Aristotle and Aquinas and Hume and Hegel ended up with such different views of the world – they all started from different places, and there's no way of 'proving' which starting point is the right one. (It could be human flourishing, personal experience, human reason, divine revelation, the history of the world, or lots of other things.) I don't think it's true that just one of them was obviously right while the others were all idiots. Say what you like about philosophers, but they weren't idiots.

That doesn't mean that everyone's right, and nobody's wrong. It just means that you can't always 'prove' they are. Instead of thinking that we can prove what we believe, and that the only reason Hegel didn't agree with us was that he was stupid, I think we're better off admitting that our starting points, our assumptions, aren't obvious to everybody, because they aren't. Then, when we've seen what conclusions our assumptions lead us to, we can consider how well they fit with all the evidence we have. And, if they don't fit that well, whether we might even need to change our assumptions.

* * *

It's a Hercule Poirot thing, really.

When I was a child, I used to love reading about Agatha Christie's famous detective, with his egg-shaped head and neat moustache and little grey cells, who often found significance in the fact that Mr So-and-So had a beard, or that it was sunny on the day of the murder, and who always solved the mystery at the end. When I was about ten, the series was on TV at nine o'clock at night, and I used to lie awake for ages, because I'd watch the first half and then have to go to bed, while still trying to solve the murder. More than once, my parents had to come upstairs and tell me who the murderer was, so I would stop trying to work it out and go to sleep.

Poirot didn't have the luxury of proving things mathematically or scientifically. He couldn't solve mysteries by equations, and he couldn't do a controlled experiment, putting a suspect in a room with the victim, handing him the murder weapon, and then watching to see if he killed him. Instead, he had to collect evidence, or clues, which would point to one explanation as being simpler, more complete and more coherent than the others. In other words, he had to demonstrate things by reconstruction (like history or archaeology), rather than by definition (like maths), or by repetition (like chemistry). If he succeeded, a jury would agree that the case was made beyond reasonable doubt. But Poirot couldn't move beyond reasonable doubt using equations or experiments, so he had to use explanations. And the best explanation won.

I think we know things in the same way as Hercule Poirot. We gather evidence, we put forward various explanations (or 'hypotheses' if you're a scientist, or 'stories' if you're a post-modern critic), and then we see which explanation includes all the evidence, and does so more simply and coherently than the others. In Agatha Christie's masterpiece, *The Murder of Roger Ackroyd*, almost all the evidence points to one explanation, but Poirot refuses to accept it, because one thing, an anonymous phone call, doesn't make any sense within that explanation. The hypothesis is simple and coherent, but it doesn't include all the evidence, so he goes on looking . . . and, of course, solves the case with spectacular flair at the end.

We reconstruct the past in the same way. We tell stories – or produce hypotheses, or explanations – that account for all the evidence, and if there are pieces of information that don't fit, then we have to adjust our story, or bin it altogether. This is how we worked out there was a Hundred Years War, and that Hannibal invaded Italy on elephants.

Sometimes, odd pieces of information don't fit, and theories have to be adjusted hugely to account for the evidence. When John F. Kennedy was shot in 1963, most people believed in the 'lone-gunman theory', in which Lee Harvey Oswald shot Kennedy on his own. But as time went on, bits of evidence turned up that didn't fit the theory, and the simple explanation (lone gunman) proved incapable of including all the evidence (the Zapruder film, the magic bullet, the man on the grassy knoll, and so on). So people came up with different explanations. In 1979, the House Select Committee on Assassinations decided that it was a 'probable conspiracy', which seems about right, if a bit vague. This opened the door to Oliver Stone's 1991 movie *JFK*, which I watched when I was fourteen, and even then found a bit far-fetched – it included all the tricky pieces of evidence, but incorporated them into a massively complex paranoid fantasy involving the Mafia, the CIA, Lyndon Johnson, Richard Nixon, Bell Helicopters, Fidel

Castro, and basically anybody and everybody who had had power in America in the 1960s. Compelling, entertaining, sinister, but complete nonsense, even to a fourteen-year-old.

Now I don't think it really matters whether or not the Select Committee were right, even though I think they probably were. The point I'm making is that all three of these reconstructions are explaining the past using stories, hypotheses, whatever you want to call them – and that we generally prefer explanations that are simple, comprehensive and coherent, just like Poirot did. Scientists love to use the word 'elegant' in this context. To me, this seems to fit with how we know things in normal life: it's how we decide who tapped us on the shoulder (the person next to me is nearest, but they don't know me, and people who haven't met me before don't generally do that), and how we decide which child hit the other one first, and whether unemployment is going up or down, and everything.

* * *

Two years ago, my wife Rachel and I were living in a third-floor flat in a slightly rough area, and she woke with a start in the middle of the night.

'Andrew, wake up! There's someone in our building!'

Rachel often woke up thinking things like that. I remember once she started searching for a baby under the bed, because she had just had a dream, and was convinced she had left it there. So I didn't pay this latest false alarm any attention, and mumbled, 'No, there isn't. Go back to sleep.'

Usually, that was enough to pacify her, but not that night. She tossed and turned for a minute, and then got up and wandered around the bedroom, still convinced that some mysterious roof-jumper was in our building. I just rolled over and started dozing off again. The simplest explanation was that she had imagined a noise in her dream, and had been scared by it.

Rachel went over to the window and opened the curtain. Instantly, she gave a little shriek, and shouted, 'Andrew, Andrew! The police are outside!'

Now I was annoyed, because her waking dream was going too far. I got up and, rather dazed, shuffled to the window, more to pull her back to bed than anything else. But when I looked, I was astonished to see a police car on the street, with flashlights pointing directly up at our roof, and a fire engine with a turntable ladder climbing up the side of the building. The police were shouting up to us that there was somebody running across the roofs of the houses, and that we should tell them if we had seen or heard anyone. Still half-asleep, I felt a mixture of fright and embarrassment; fresh evidence had come to light, and Rachel's idea had just become a bit more likely. Fortunately, there was still nothing to suggest that this man was in our building, or anything like that.

The police were keen to talk to us, so I put on my white dressing gown and went down the stairs of our building towards the ground floor. (White dressing gowns always seem like a good idea for bedrooms and spas, but if you're talking to the police in the middle of the night, you soon feel rather stupid in them.) Rachel was still insistent that the roof-jumper could be in the building, but I knew this was the fear talking, so I confidently marched down the staircase, eager to get rid of the police and go back to sleep.

I was about halfway down, between the ground floor and the flat where the Polish guys lived, when I became aware that there was a person crouching in the shadows of our stairwell. I couldn't see their face in the dark, but it didn't look like either of the Polish guys, and I very much doubted it was Amy from the ground floor, because – well, that's not the sort of things single girls generally do at one in the morning. Instantly, Rachel's 'he's in our building' explanation came into sharp focus. Feeling like an idiot, I said, 'Hello?'

'I can't let you past,' a man's voice said. This wasn't the ideal start. I didn't know if he was armed, drugged, dangerous, or what.

'What's going on?'

'Yeah, I'm really sorry about this, but I can't let you past. I'm just waiting for the police to go, and then you can do what you like.'

Rachel was more awake than I was, and she said what both of us were thinking: 'But – but you're in our house.'

The man thought about this for a moment. It was obviously a social situation that was as new to him as it was to us. 'Yeah. Sorry.'

'How did you get in here?'

'I got on the roof at number sixty-four. Do you know Trish and Mick?'

This was too much. It was bad enough having a strange man crouching in our stairwell, let alone that Rachel's explanation had been proved right, but to be asked whether we knew Trish and Mick, as if it would make everything all right if we did, was verging on the surreal. This was the most polite roof-jumper I had ever heard of. 'No, we don't! But what are you doing here? How did you get into the building?'

'I came in through the open window of the flat upstairs.' I wondered what the Polish guys would think when they got back home and discovered that. 'Then I came down here, and now I'm just waiting for the police to go.'

'Well, I'm sorry, but I'm going to go to the front door now, and I don't mind if you go outside, but you can't stay here.' I said it more confidently than I felt it, but found myself moving towards the door, still in my white dressing gown.

To my surprise, he let me, and then followed me. I turned the handle.

It was one of the biggest anticlimaxes of my life. The police, in an attempt to find him, had gone round to the other side of our building, and were nowhere to be seen. Our new acquaintance, sensing freedom, made a run for it, sprinting off down the road with a final apology to us for the inconvenience. If I had been more awake, or a former policeman, or wearing anything other than a robe, I might have done something. But I wasn't, so I didn't. The police were very understanding.

I tell that story because I think it illustrates the view of knowledge that I've been talking about. When I was in bed, I was faced with a set of data, and came up with an explanation: Rachel had heard a random bump and was freaking out about it, without good reason. When she went to the window and saw the police, new evidence emerged that made her theory a bit more likely, but it was still ridiculous to think the guy was actually in our building. When I saw the person crouching in the shadows, her explanation suddenly looked very likely indeed, although not certain. (It could have been a random bump, the police could have been mistaken, or one of the Polish guys could have been playing a prank on the other one.) But when I spoke to him, and he told me his bizarre story, I regarded Rachel's story as being proved beyond reasonable doubt. I cannot 'prove' that the bump that awoke Rachel was made by him – there aren't any experiments or equations that could do that. But with explanations, I can 'know' that it was.

So I think we know things by finding the simplest, most comprehensive and most coherent explanation for the evidence. And I think this view avoids the two extremes I've been talking about. It avoids the Matrix extreme (we can only know about ourselves and our experiences), and it also avoids the Nottingham High School extreme. (Remember my friend John's teenagers? – if it can't be proved on a blackboard or in a lab, it can't be known.) From where I'm sitting, in fact, it's a very good answer to the question: 'How do we know?'

★ ★ ★

A little while back, I was thinking this stuff through, and so I did a thought-experiment to see how it worked in practice, and wrote it all down. The thought-experiment was this: how do I know that I ate cornflakes for breakfast this morning?

Phenomenalists would have to say: you don't. (They're still trying to work out whether there is a world out there, let alone breakfast.) But hardline positivists would have to say that too. I can't prove that I ate cornflakes by definition, and I can't do an experiment to prove it either – at least, not without cutting myself open, which I'm unlikely to be keen on. So maybe I can't know whether I ate cornflakes or not.

But I think that gives away too much. A bit of common sense, and the view of knowledge I've been talking about, might combine to work like this:

(1) I am aware of a whole bunch of evidence. My memory, which is usually reliable, tells me that I ate cornflakes. I don't feel hungry, which I normally would by twelve o'clock. The cornflake packet now contains fewer cornflakes than it did yesterday. And my wife Rachel tells me she washed up a bowl containing the remains of cornflakes after I had gone to work.

(2) I can think of at least two different explanations for the evidence. (i) I ate cornflakes this morning (and didn't wash up). (ii) My memory is playing tricks on me, which it occasionally does; I ate toast instead, which is why I do not feel hungry; Rachel ate a bowl of cornflakes herself, which explains the lighter packet and the dirty bowl; she then either forgot about it or lied about it.

(3) I compare the different explanations, to see if either of them is noticeably simpler or more complete or more coherent than the others. In this case, option (i) is obviously more likely. It is simpler and requires fewer unknown causes than option (ii), it includes all the evidence, and it is internally coherent. As such, using an explanation-based approach, I can 'know' that I ate cornflakes this morning.

Thank goodness for that.

⋆ ⋆ ⋆

I think this is how pretty much all knowledge works. It's why scientists believe in evolution (which they haven't observed) and a Big Bang (when they weren't there) and quarks (which they can't see). It's how we know that I ate cornflakes and Shakespeare wrote plays and Hannibal invaded Italy and George Washington was President. One, we identify what the evidence is; two, we establish the possible explanations; and three, we see which one explains the evidence more completely, simply and coherently than the others.

If this is right, then we wouldn't expect to be able to 'prove' the existence of God, as the teenagers in Nottingham wanted John to do. We can't 'prove' that Caesar existed, or even that we exist, let alone that God does. But that doesn't mean we have to throw up our hands in frustration, and announce that we'll never know either way. That would give far too much away. Instead, we can identify what evidence might be relevant to the question, establish what explanations have been put forward for it, and see which one works best.

And the first piece of evidence that needs explaining is very simple. There is a world.

3.
GALACTIC ROULETTE: HOW DID WE GET HERE?

It's hard to put into words how boring I used to find physics lessons. On my first ever day at boarding school, our timetable said we had double physics followed by maths in the run-up to lunch, which was pretty bad, but it turned out that Dr Evans was somewhat vague about timekeeping, so we ended up with triple physics, which was unthinkably dull. It wasn't a great start to my relationship with the subject, and things went downhill from there.

The classrooms and everything in them were always grey. They also had a rather stale smell to them, either because the windows were tiny and never opened, or because of those weird, inexplicably long and thin black taps that sat in the middle of the desks, dripping tepid chemical-infused water onto the enamel beneath. Occasionally, a lab assistant would emerge from inside one of the walk-in cupboards, carrying a piece of equipment, and we would wonder whether he lived there. Other than that, though, we would just sit still, hoping for an experiment to break the tedium of listening, even though the experiments were almost as boring as the listening. I remember one lesson in three years – the one where the class clown gets plugged into the van de Graaff generator and gradually morphs into Albert Einstein – but other than that, physics was interminably dull. The only lesson that was nearly as boring was chemistry, but there was a bit of natural light in the chemistry department, and Mr Ramsden used to go off on tangents all the time rather than talking about the subject, so it wasn't quite as bad.

I say all this to show you that I'm not a science geek. I hated science at school, especially physics, and I stopped studying it as early as I could. So I find it quite ironic that I'm now writing a chapter about it. Because, it turns out, physics as a subject – as distinct from the lessons at school, which I will never defend – is mind-bendingly interesting, and helps us engage with one of the most important questions we can ever ask: How did we get here?

* * *

People have been trying to work out how our universe got here for thousands of years. So it's kind of surprising that if you ask around, there are really only three types of explanation: luck, or a multiverse (which is a theory that exists because of how unlikely the 'luck' theory is), or a creator of some sort. I think that's quite an interesting fact. I mean, you can talk to the man on the street, or study a religious text of some sort, or read high-powered scientists like Rees, Carr, Tegmark and co, but you won't get anything other than these three types of view (unless it's a combination of two of them). Either our universe is the result of a massively fortunate cosmic accident (luck), or there are billions of universes out there that we can't observe (multiverse), or there's some sort of god or intelligent mind who made it (creator).

I don't know which one you lean towards, but it's pretty much got to be one of those three, whether you're religious, or an atheist, or you don't really care. And I think that's fascinating. If Dr Evans had taught us about all this in physics lessons, I would have found them a lot less grey.

* * *

Most people today agree that the universe had a beginning. A few decades ago, that wouldn't have been true, but it is now. Great scientists like Albert Einstein, before he plugged himself into the van de Graaff generator, used to believe in a 'static universe', until a Belgian astronomer called Georges Lemaître, who was a Catholic priest as well as a physics professor, came up with a new theory. In 1927, he argued that the universe was expanding, and when Einstein disagreed with him about it, Lemaître accused him of being abominable at physics (which may have been a little harsh). He then argued that the universe started in a tiny point, which he called 'the cosmic egg exploding at the moment of creation', and by the time he died in 1966, so much research had confirmed his theory that it was widely accepted in the scientific community.

Sadly, we don't call it the Cosmic Egg theory any more, because in 1949 another scientist was making fun of it on the radio, and he used a phrase that caught on more quickly. So these days we call it the Big Bang. And for most (though by no means all) scientists today, it makes it look pretty clear that the universe had a beginning.

I don't know whether you believe in the Big Bang. You might prefer to believe in an eternal universe that has always been like it is now, or perhaps a universe that was created much more recently and without an explosion, or possibly you favour one of the latest fashions in cosmology – the idea that the universe existed before the Big Bang, perhaps going through a succession of big bangs and big crunches. But if you accept the conclusions of almost all scientists today, then you will end up with a universe that began 13.7 billion years ago with an explosion that we now call the Big Bang. And if that's true, it prompts two questions: what caused this explosion? And what caused stars, planets, water and life to form afterwards?

In other words, how did we get here?

* * *

A lot of people would say, nothing caused it. There was a Big Bang (at least one), and we don't know why; the universe is very big, so it was bound to produce life somewhere; we're just lucky, so stop worrying about it.

I used to think that was fair enough. But when I eventually overcame my phobia of physics and started reading into it, I came across some amazing things which make this explanation totally absurd. For stars and planets to be possible in the first place, before we've started trying to work out how life got here, there are fifteen numbers that all have to be exactly what they are. (Dr Evans would have called them 'constants', but I'll call them 'numbers'.) I'm talking about numbers like the size of the strong and weak nuclear forces, the speed at which the universe first expanded, the amount of gravity we have, the size of the universe, and so on – fifteen different numbers that have to be *exactly* what they are for stars and planets to form, to the tune of one part in a million (and in some cases, one part in a million million). Forget *life* for a minute: I'm talking about how planets are even possible. And I discovered that, if it was only down to chance, the universe was unthinkably unlikely to produce stars, let alone carbon-based planets with moons and mountains and ozone and oak trees. That's why scientists, looking at the astonishing fact of our universe, use phrases like 'fine-tuning' and 'cosmic welcome mat', and even say things like, 'The universe looks as if it knew we were coming.' It really does.

Let me bore you with a few examples, because these really blew my mind when I first found out about them.

One: if the ratio between the strong nuclear constant and the electromagnetic constant was different by one part in ten million billion, there wouldn't be any stars. You don't have to know anything about physics to see that this is fairly remarkable.

Two: If the balance between the gravity constant and the electromagnetic constant was altered by one part in 10^{40}, the types of stars that would form would be incapable of sustaining planets with life. That's ten with forty noughts after it, which is roughly equivalent to covering America, and a billion other continents the same size, with piles of coins stretching to the moon, hiding one red coin in one of the piles, and a blindfolded friend picking it out by chance. (My thanks to Hugh Ross for that illustration: www.reasons.org.)

Three: I was talking just now about the leading scientist who first used the term 'Big Bang' on the radio. His name was Fred Hoyle, and he said that the fine-tuning of nuclear energy levels which are needed to produce carbon made it look as if 'a superintellect has monkeyed with physics as well as with chemistry and biology', and that this discovery had rocked his atheism more than anything else. (I'm not saying it should have, by the way; I'm just telling you what he said.)

Four: the amount of entropy (basically, disorder) in the universe is so accurately prescribed that one Oxford scientist, Sir Roger Penrose – if you've got a name like that, you're bound to be an Oxford scientist, aren't you? – said the improbability was too big to write down, because 'if I were to put one zero on each elementary particle in the Universe, I still could not write the number down in full'. Wow.

And so on, and so on.

I was trying to work this all out in my head one day, so I imagined a game of galactic roulette. I pictured fifteen massive roulette wheels in the sky, each of which had a million numbers on them, representing all the different constants that have to fit together for the solar system to be here. Then I imagined someone spinning the first wheel, representing the gravity constant, and seeing the ball bounce and bounce and bounce past all the million numbers, until it landed on exactly the right one for our universe to be like it is. Then I imagined them spinning the second wheel, for the size of the strong nuclear constant, and again, seeing the ball bounce past all these hundreds of thousands of alternative values, until it landed once again on the right number.

I imagined them doing this fourteen times, with the ball bouncing around each time before landing in the perfect place, and then on the fifteenth one something going slightly wrong, and the ball landing on the number next door to the right one, and the entire universe collapsing and imploding as a result, sucking the Horsehead Nebula and the Andromeda Galaxy and the Alps and the Cook Islands into a vortex of non-existence. I saw in my mind's eye the mountains being hoovered up, and the oceans boiling, and cars flying upside down through the air and crashing into concrete bridges and bursting into flames, and the New York skyscrapers being levelled and covering the city with rubble, like in a nuclear holocaust, all because one of the numbers was out by one part in a million. And I began to realize that these fifteen numbers, all of which have to be exactly what they are for a universe like this to exist, made the galactic roulette idea completely impossible. I just couldn't believe that there was one Big Bang, caused and guided by nobody at all, and that it just happened to produce a universe so staggeringly suitable for life. To be honest, I couldn't imagine who would.

* * *

Most scientists don't, of course. That's why the other two explanations – the multiverse and the creator – creep into the discussion so often. Some scientists believe in a multiverse of some sort, some lean towards a creator of some sort, and a few believe in both. But I think it's safe to say two things: neither a multiverse nor a creator are proper scientific theories, and they only get brought up in the first place because saying, 'It just happened that way' doesn't really cut the mustard.

Even if we stop there, I think that's remarkable. The universe had a beginning; the more we look at it, the more we realize that we can't understand it without going beyond the universe to find an explanation; and when we do, there are only two real alternatives – either there are billions of other universes that we can't see, or a creator that we can't see. Even the most diehard atheists admit that these are the only two possibilities. Not just that, but since neither of them can be demonstrated scientifically, all of us have to decide between them for other reasons.

So I have to decide how to continue with this chapter. The most impressive-looking option would be to quote a long list of prize-winning scientists who agree with me, produce great quotations about fine-tuning and the Creator's aim, and misquote Stephen Hawking a few times to make it look like all scientists basically believe in God. But I don't want to do that. Not just because there are plenty of books like that out there, but because I'm not convinced that this is even a scientific question.

That might sound a bit odd, but think about it. Neither the multiverse nor the creator explanations can be tested scientific-ally, as the most recent major scientific book on the subject (Bernard Carr's *Universe or Multiverse?*) explains. It would be like Romeo scientifically proving the existence of either Shakespeare, or of all the characters in the other plays. (If you press the analogy, I guess Shakespeare would be like the Creator, and the characters in other plays would be parallel universes.)

Do you see what I mean? Science can *raise* the question: 'How did we get here?' by showing us how fine-tuned the universe is, but ultimately it can't *answer* it. And the way I know this is, when you get to this issue in the scientific literature, you find that top scientists, whatever their beliefs, start using words like 'prefer' or 'suppose' or 'speculate', because they know it's beyond the scope of their research. I just read an article in this month's *Scientific American*, in which the authors said they believed in the multiverse because a supernatural designer would be outside the realms of science – which may be true, but it isn't a very good reason to argue against it. (As the philosopher Alvin Plantinga puts it, that's a bit like a drunk man arguing that his car keys must be under a street lamp, because he wouldn't be able to find them if they weren't in the light.) So as much as I love scientists, I don't think their personal preferences on this issue are even relevant.

Instead, I want to quote an illustration. If you've read into this debate much, you've probably come across it already: it comes from the Canadian philosopher John Leslie, and it gets quoted by people on both sides of the aisle. I think it's very clever, and when I first came across it, it really helped me think more clearly about these things.

Imagine a man sentenced to death by firing squad. Fifty expert marksmen are lined up in a row, aiming their rifles at his heart, and as the sergeant shouts, 'Ready, Aim, Fire!', he hears a loud bang. Blindfolded, he doesn't know what has happened, but with the passing of time he becomes aware that he is not in fact dead, but somehow, all fifty marksmen have missed. It will not be long before the question occurs to him: 'How did I survive?' There are three possible ways for him to think at this point.

He might think to himself, 'Everybody missed. That's kind of surprising. But if they hadn't missed, then I wouldn't be here thinking about it, because I'd be dead. In fact, the only outcome I could possibly have experienced is this one. So although it's odd, it doesn't require an explanation. Time for a drink, I think!'

Alternatively, he might acknowledge how desperately unlikely it was that they all missed by chance, and consider another explanation. 'What if there are hundreds of thousands of executions taking place today? At some point, it is possible that at least one group of marksmen will all miss – and maybe it just happens that I am the fortunate survivor. Odd, yes; but then whoever survived would think that, wouldn't they? Onwards and upwards!'

Or finally, he might wonder as follows: 'Fifty marksmen have all missed. That is unimaginably unlikely – unless, that is, they all just happen to like me. Or someone has bribed them. Or got them drunk. Whatever the reason, it looks like there's something deliberate about all this. It looks like someone, an intelligent being of some sort, has engineered this situation to let me survive. I wonder who?'

* * *

The other day I was thinking about all this, and my mind wandered to Antony Flew.

Antony Flew was a very interesting guy. He was one of the world's leading atheist philosophers for almost fifty years, and I studied him when I was at university. He wrote books and articles about how we should presume atheism was right, and how there was no proper evidence for belief in God, and he debated publicly against Christians. In that way, he was kind of a less angry, pre-9/11 version of Chris Hitchens. His first atheist paper, 'Theology and Falsification', was the most widely reprinted philosophical paper of the twentieth century.

Now, it's not every day that leading academics announce that they've been wrong about something very important for their entire career. That probably explains why it was such a bombshell when, on 9 December 2004, Associated Press ran a story headlined: 'Famous Atheist Now Believes in God: One of World's Leading Atheists Now Believes in God, More or Less, Based on Scientific Evidence.' This provoked all sorts of interest and comments, some of which were pretty nasty, as we'll see in a minute. But Antony Flew explained that, for his entire career, he had committed himself to following the evidence wherever it leads, and that it had now led him to believe that there was a god. I was intrigued to find out what had made him say this, so I bought his book, *There Is A God: How the World's Most Notorious Atheist Changed His Mind*, to find out.

The answer was quite extraordinary. Here's what he said:

> Why do I believe this, given that I expounded and defended atheism for more than a half century? The short answer is this: this is the world picture, as I see it, that has emerged from modern science. Science spotlights three dimensions of nature that point to God. The first is the fact that nature obeys laws. The second is the dimension of life, of intelligently organized and purpose-driven beings, which arose from matter. The third is the very existence of nature.

He then went on to explain each of these three arguments in more detail.

I had studied him as an atheist philosopher at university, so I found it hard to believe what I was reading. But he seemed pretty clear about it. The laws of nature, he said, pointed to there being a divine mind behind the laws that enabled the universe to exist. The universe seems to have known we were coming, he continued, and this should provoke the same reaction as we would have if we walked into a hotel room to find our favourite CDs, books, fragrances, paintings, food and drinks everywhere we turned. The multiverse is a silly theory that, like a blunderbuss, explains everything and nothing. The Big Bang shows that the universe had a beginning, which tips the balance of probabilities in favour of God. On and on he went, giving reason after reason for believing in a god, based not on personal experience or preference, but on scientific evidence.

Now I have to say that none of this means he's right. And it's not like he became a Christian or a Muslim or anything; before he died he still had some serious questions about revelation and stuff like that. Yet the fact that someone with fifty years of atheist philosophical writings behind him could change his mind, and say that scientific evidence pointed to a god, ought to make people of all perspectives consider his argument. I certainly did.

Unfortunately, this isn't quite what happened. Instead, all sorts of people who should probably have known better started accusing him of abandoning atheism because he was old and couldn't think straight, or was old and afraid of death, or was old and had been manipulated by other people, or just wanted to make money. It was very sad, actually. It wasn't just ranting bloggers, but serious atheist academics who came out of the woodwork to denounce his departure from atheism as the act of a confused old man – as if eighty-one was too old to think straight. (Have you ever counted up the Nobel Prize winners who have been in their eighties? I did just now, and I couldn't believe how many there were, and in 2007, the economics prize was won by a guy who was ninety.) All of which made me wonder: why are people saying these things about him, rather than responding to his arguments? You wouldn't get away with that in economics, would you? Imagine it: 'I know your arguments look strong, but you're old, so shut up.' What is going on here?

★ ★ ★

You can get into trouble for asking questions. I guess the question that got Antony Flew into trouble with his fellow atheists, in a nutshell, was: 'How did we get here?' Lots of people are happy these days to say, 'Stop asking that; we just did. The universe is just here. Lump it.' But that's why questions have such power. As soon as you ask what the options are – luck, multiverse or creator (or the last two together) – and have to start deciding between them, you realize what Antony Flew realized. The scientific evidence for a creator may well be stronger than you thought.

I was talking about this recently with a guy who had read Victor Stenger, the feisty atheist and professor at the University of Colorado. Victor Stenger had written an article that had convinced him the galactic roulette argument was bunk, and improbabilities were not as surprising as they seemed. His argument was, if you shuffle a pack of fifty-two cards and then deal them all out, the probability of any particular order of cards coming out (say, three of spades, then eight of clubs, then king of hearts, and so on) will be astronomically low: 1 in 10^{68}. That might sound improbable, but we know that it isn't, because whichever combination of cards had come out would have been equally unlikely. It's the same with the constants in the universe. They look improbable, but they're not.

It sounded like a good argument at first, but then I started thinking about it, and I realized the analogy wasn't quite right.

From what we know about physics, it appears that the vast majority of combinations of numbers – and possibly, all except the combination in our universe – would not result in life at all. So it's more like somebody shuffling the pack of cards, specifying in advance the exact order in which all fifty-two of them would be dealt (three of spades, eight of clubs, king of hearts, and so on), betting me a million pounds that he'd get it right, and then seeing the cards coming out in exactly that order. If that happened to me, it would make me assume either that the pack wasn't shuffled at all and the dealer had a great memory, or that a magic trick of some sort had been performed. In other words, I would look at the massive improbability and conclude that intelligence was at work. I certainly wouldn't shrug my shoulders and decide it was no more unlikely than any other outcome. (Nor, of course, would I conclude that billions of card dealers had tried doing this, and I just happened to be there when it all worked out in order. People who think like this in real life tend to get duped more often than most.)

One last analogy, once again from the philosopher John Leslie, and then I'll wrap up. He imagines a man fishing in a cloudy lake, and catching a fish measuring 23.2576 inches long. On the face of it, he says, there is nothing at all unlikely about that; all fishes have some length or other. But what if he then discovers that his fishing apparatus could only accept fishes of 23.2576 inches long, plus or minus one part in a million? Suddenly the picture would change. A number that had not appeared at all relevant would become quite amazing to him. He might well conclude that the fish had been planted there by someone who wanted him to have a fish supper.

* * *

I ended the last chapter by saying that the existence of our world is a piece of evidence that needs an explanation, and in this chapter I've described the three possible explanations: luck, multiverse and creator. Personally, I find the 'luck' explanation completely unbelievable, and I've pointed towards some reasons why I've come to believe that a creator is more likely than a multiverse. Before moving on, though, I want to make two comments, in case it sounds like I'm going too far too fast.

The first one is this: none of these arguments can prove either a multiverse or a creator. It's quite important to be clear on this, I think, because people can talk sometimes as if their view is scientifically proven, when actually it's a conclusion they've reached that is ultimately beyond the reaches of science. (Again, Romeo can be sure about Juliet, but not about Shakespeare, and certainly not about Hamlet or Macbeth.) Personally, I reckon the question: 'How did we get here?' is better answered by a creator than a multiverse – I find it easier to believe in one unseen, unprovable entity than billions of unseen, unprovable entities – but lots of people see it the other way round, so I'm not saying I can prove it. I can't.

Secondly, even if we do conclude that a creator is more likely than a multiverse, this doesn't tell us anything about what such a creator might be like (and it certainly doesn't prove that the God of Judaism, Christianity or Islam is real). Religious believers can get muddled on this sometimes, as if we can go science → creator → God of Abraham in three easy steps, which of course we can't. Science and philosophy, not to mention theology, just don't work like that.

Having said that, thinking this stuff through convinced me of four important things. One: the fine-tuning of our universe needs a good explanation. Two: of the three explanations, only two are feasible. Three: both of them involve believing in an unseen, unprovable reality beyond our universe, whether a creator (one reality) or a multiverse (billions of realities). Science can't prove or disprove either of them.

And four? Even if scientists were to discover causes for the fine-tuning of the universe that could be expressed purely mathematically, and in terms of physics, it would make me even more suspicious that somebody somewhere had skewed the numbers in our favour.

★ ★ ★

So how else might we decide between God and the multiverse, if we even can? Is there any other evidence that might help?

I think there is. Right now, as your eyes read these words, and as the blobs of ink you're looking at are translated into information by the two-pint squidgy grey thing behind your face, and as your thoughts wander on to what you're going to do next, you're encountering another piece of evidence to consider. The mind.

4.
MIND OVER MATTER: WHY DO YOU THINK?

Imagine the earth without life.

It's quite hard, actually. When I try, it takes me several attempts. First, I imagine the earth without animal life, but for reasons I can't fully explain, probably something to do with *Jurassic Park*, there are always dinosaurs roaming around in my imagination. So I have to go back and take them all out, like doing CGI in reverse. Now I've managed to rid the earth of all animal life, only to find that there are trees everywhere, so I have to go back and edit the picture again. It's a struggle, but it can be done. Then I look at my imaginary world, and notice with horror that it's covered in grass – sweeping plains of it, stretching in all directions, looking rather eerie and desolate without the dinosaurs or the wildebeest. Evidently, getting away from the picture of a blue-green planet is not very easy to do.

At this point, I adopt a change of strategy. Instead of starting with the earth and stripping off the layers of life which are so familiar to me, I start with a mental picture of another planet, like Mars, and adjust it. To be honest, I don't really know what Mars looks like, but it's much easier to imagine than a lifeless earth. So I start with Mars, with its mountains and valleys, and I add the Grand Canyon and the occasional desert (being careful not to allow desert foxes, or rattlesnakes, to sneak in through the back door and send me back to square one). It's all going well, for a while, until I have to add oceans. For some reason, putting lifeless oceans, and rivers and lakes without any fish, on to my imaginary Mars/Earth presents me with a real problem, although it's easier than picturing the earth without grass. After much effort, and some exhausting mental gymnastics, I end up with a lifeless earth that I am almost happy with.

I mention all this because, scientists say, around 3.8 billion years ago planet earth looked a bit like that. From all we can tell, earth back then was a barren landscape of rocks, volcanoes, mountains and oceans, with highly acidic rainfall and lots of thunderstorms. Kind of like Mordor without the orcs.

Lots more could be said, but I just want to mention a couple of things about this primeval earth that I think are important. Obviously, there is no life. There is no consciousness, let alone self-consciousness, on earth, and there are no thoughts. There is no such thing as an organism – no animals, plants, bacteria, or whatever. Cells do not exist. There are no genes or chromosomes, and neither DNA nor RNA exists. In fact, there is no such thing as information on the whole of planet earth (sounds weird, but stop and think about what information is, and you'll see that it's true). The physical world consists entirely of matter: unsorted, non-reproducing groups of atoms and molecules that happen to form lumps of rock or salt or gas or water. Minerals. That's it.

* * *

3.8 billion years is a long time, but in the grand scheme of things, it's not as long as we might think. I used to assume that, if you just gave it a few billion years on earth, the emergence of living, information-transmitting, reproducing creatures was pretty much guaranteed. But then I did some basic calculations, and I worked out that if you started a monkey typing randomly at three keystrokes per second, and told him to type the word 'consciousness', it would take him about three and a half billion years. It suddenly became a bit more unlikely to me that time and chance could create life on their own.

* * *

Now fast forward 3.8 billion years, back to the present day. In the amount of time it would take the monkey to type 'consciousness', an entirely mineral earth has produced the unthinkable: a living cell, even the simplest of which (the tiniest bacterial cell) comprises 100,000 million atoms, with thousands of chemical factories inside it, and with a degree of complexity that dwarfs the most complicated machines that humans have ever produced. Not only that, but these tiny living cells have found a way of replicating themselves, passing information from one generation to the next, using a massively intricate four-letter digital code called DNA. The result is that our lifeless earth has been transformed into an astonishingly diverse planet, filled with all kinds of life, and in particular one creature with the capacity for abstract thought, language, art, story, ethical dilemmas, daydreams and discovery. Human beings.

That is remarkable. In my view, it's so remarkable that it needs an explanation. The existence of life, cells, information, thoughts, self-consciousness, things like that – they're all pieces of evidence that we need to consider when we think about God, the multiverse and everything.

In essence, I think the question boils down to this. Why do you think? Is it because minerals somehow turned into living things which became more complicated and eventually resulted in a being who talked and laughed and wondered why it was there? Are thoughts and emotions entirely physical, chemical, mineral? (That's basically what materialism is: the belief that everything is matter.) Or are thoughts, emotions and information different types of things from minerals, and might the fact that we encounter them in our universe point to an ultimate mind, a creator of some sort?

* * *

When I was thirteen, I got really into Douglas Adams's *Hitchhiker's Guide to the Galaxy* series. (If you haven't read them, they're a series of comedy books about an ordinary guy who gets caught up in space travel after the earth is destroyed to make room for a bypass, and they're hilarious. Then again, if you haven't read them, or seen or heard one of the radio or screen adaptations, you probably haven't lived.) Before I read them, I don't think I'd ever laughed out loud at a book before, but then a few people in my school got into them, and we started quoting them to one another all the time, laughing hysterically like thirteen-year-olds do when they're in on a joke and you're not. In the dormitory at night, someone would do the routine where the computer tells everyone that the meaning of life is forty-two, and everyone would fall about laughing. Or I'd walk down the corridor and say, 'In the beginning, the universe was created,' and Stewart Morris would say, 'This has made a lot of people very angry, and has been widely regarded as a bad move.' Then we'd both carry on to our lessons, giggling. Good times.

So far as I was concerned, Douglas Adams was a genius. Not just for *The Hitchhiker's Guide*, although that was amazing. His little spoof dictionary, *The Meaning of Liff*, defined the word 'Corriearklet', which is really a place in Scotland, as: 'The moment at which two people approaching from opposite ends of a long passageway, recognize each other and immediately pretend they haven't. This is to avoid the ghastly embarrassment of having to continue recognizing each other the whole length of the corridor.' The man was inspired.

I had dinner with him once, when I was at university, because he was the guest speaker at an event I'd been invited to. It was quite weird, because at one point I found myself in a conversation with him and Germaine Greer, which is pretty intimidating when you're a teenager, and you're not that funny, and you're not a radical feminist – you find yourself making the most ridiculous conversation, just so you feel like you've got something to say, which (it sadly turns out) you haven't. When we finally got to his speech, which was the reason I was there, I remember being a bit disappointed with it, because his main joke was an anecdote I'd heard loads of times which obviously wasn't true, and which he could have pulled off the internet for all I know. I still count it a privilege to have met him, though, and I remain a huge fan of his writing.

But one of his most famous throwaway remarks – at least, famous since a friend of his quoted it while dedicating a book that sold a million copies – really bothered me when I first read it, and it sums up pretty well the mind/matter conversation I'm talking about. He said, 'Isn't it enough to see that a garden is beautiful without having to believe that there are fairies at the bottom of it too?'

Douglas Adams called himself a radical atheist, and this was his way of saying that belief in a creator was unnecessary. If you come across a beautiful garden, then the right response is to appreciate its beauty for its own sake, rather than inventing all sorts of mythical creatures and pretending they live there. That, he argued, is what people do when they believe in God. They encounter a world that is very beautiful, filled with incredibly complex and magnificent creatures, and what they should do is appreciate it for what it is. But instead, they invent fairies – gods – to hide all over it, in the branches of the trees and under the toadstools, and then they worship these gods, when they should be focusing on the beauty. This, Douglas Adams was saying, is ridiculous. Why not just admire the garden?

You have to be careful with parables, though. They can backfire. Here's what it made me think: of course a beautiful garden would not make me believe in fairies (which is probably why no sane adult in the world believes in fairies). But it might make me believe in a *gardener*. Wouldn't you think? A beautiful garden might well make me believe that someone of intelligence and skill – in other words, some sort of *mind* – had given their time to planting, ordering and cultivating this particular patch of land, so that it became a beautiful garden rather than a tumbledown scrubland.

That's the whole point. When we find matter in an unsorted, unproductive mess, we don't tend to imagine that intelligent beings are responsible. Left to their own devices, things in nature tend to get more disordered: gardens grow weeds, snowmen melt, bedrooms become messy, bicycles rust, and so on. So when we find an ugly piece of land where the grass is overgrown and the flowers are dying, we generally conclude that nobody's been looking after it. There is no mind supervising the matter.

Beautiful gardens, on the other hand, are a different story. They display such order and beauty that we immediately see a mind behind the matter. Nobody in their right mind walks through the gardens at Versailles and thinks they just happened to come about that way; we all know that a very skilled and intelligent gardener has been hard at work, trimming borders and arranging flowers, probably over many years. The Versailles gardens don't make you believe in fairies, but if you saw them and said you didn't believe in gardeners, you'd be laughed off the stage.

Perhaps it's the same with the earth. If you came across a place that had bucked the trend towards disorder, a place where total chaos had turned into astonishing order and beauty, rather than the other way around – where, for instance, you started with a Bang and ended up with a brain – you might think that some mind, some sort of gardener, was behind it all. Maybe Douglas Adams spoke better than he knew.

★ ★ ★

Here's another way I've thought about it. If everything in the universe began with some sort of supreme mind – and you don't have to call that 'god', although lots of people do – then I would expect the world to be filled with things like beauty, thought, art, music and morality, since those things come about because of minds.

On the other hand, if at the beginning of everything there was nothing but matter, then I would find it extremely surprising if all of those things had come about. Not impossible, I guess – it's *possible* that the mineral Mordor I described earlier could produce life, cells, consciousness and the rest on its own – but it would be extremely surprising. If a few billion years back we had a lifeless jumble of minerals, then I'd expect us still to have a lifeless jumble of minerals, and I certainly wouldn't expect there to be people who asked questions and wrote songs and read books like this one.

I think that's quite an important thing to bear in mind when we're asking whether mind or matter came first.

★ ★ ★

Another thing that's worth wondering about is where information came from.

Look at the size of this full stop. On that, you could fit
around 200 living cells, which are enormously complex
miniature factories that are foundational to life on earth. If
those cells were part of you, they would each have about 1,000
billion atoms in them, and they would contain 100 million
proteins, which would consist of up to 20,000 different types.
The mind boggles.

What is more extraordinary, though, is that each of those
proteins is built the way it is, and is doing the things it's doing,
because it has been told to by a string of DNA that lives in the
cell nucleus. DNA is a complicated molecule that looks kind
of like a spiral ladder, and it contains all the information
needed to tell your cells what to do – what proteins to make,
whether to be a heart muscle cell or a hair cell, what colour
to make your eyes, everything. (This isn't directly relevant,
but it's fascinating: each DNA molecule is about 2 metres
long, yet so tightly coiled that you couldn't see it if it sat
on the page in front of you. That means your body has about
12 billion miles of DNA sitting in your cells.)

The way it works is astonishing. The DNA molecule, which
lives in the cell nucleus, unzips itself down the middle, and
prints its information on to a similar type of molecule called
messenger-RNA. The messenger-RNA then carries the information out of the nucleus towards the cell's chemical factories,
which then read all the information and build the proteins
accordingly. It's like me giving a coded blueprint to a friend
in my office, who then goes outside and passes on that blueprint to a builder – except that in this case, both me and my
friend are invisibly small molecules, and the blueprint is
3.5 billion letters long, containing enough information to fill
an entire library.

So the whole diversity of life on earth is based on information, which is transferred from DNA to messenger-RNA to chemical factories, and eventually shows itself in muscles and feathers and flowers and seeds. But where did the information come from?

If you start with a mind, it's pretty straightforward. Creating and transmitting information is something that minds do all the time – you're doing it right now, as your mind translates the blobs and strokes of ink in front of you into words, and then translates the words into concepts and ideas that relate to the world you know. In fact, in some ways, you could say that communicating fresh information (as opposed to transmitting existing information, which can be done by a machine or a book or something) is a fundamental thing that minds do. So if the universe existed because of a mind, then we'd expect the world to be flooded with information at every turn. Which it is.

If you start with just matter, though, it's more complicated. The mineral Mordor I described earlier doesn't sound like it would be likely to produce information, code, language, digital data, or anything like that – and all these words are regularly used to describe what DNA is and does. For one thing, we have no example of any language or information in the world that doesn't originate with minds. Computers, mobile phones, books, even stone tablets – these things can *transfer* information, but they can't *produce* it, because that takes a mind. For another, passing information requires not just a language (which is quite a stretch in the first place), but a language that is agreed upon and understood by at least two different parties (like DNA and mRNA, or whatever.) The way I know this is that if I have a conversation with a Chinese speaker, he or she is communicating in a language, and so am I, but because we have not agreed beforehand on what each other's sounds mean, we haven't really transferred any meaningful *information* at all. In the same way, the information required to build proteins in living cells needs a code, or a language, that is agreed upon by the DNA, the mRNA and the chemical factory – and if that doesn't exist, then nothing happens.

It's also worth mentioning that information itself is not physical. The words you're reading at the moment are typed on a physical object, but the information itself can't be equated with the material objects by which it's transmitted. If you ring up a friend in a moment and tell them what this chapter is about, your voice box will have generated sound waves which convey the information, but the physical sound waves are not the same as the information (which will quickly become obvious if you accidentally ring a Chinese speaker, who will not understand a word of it – the sound waves won't actually contain any *information* so far as he or she is concerned). So how do purely material things produce non-material information? Might that suggest that information is a result of intelligence?

* * *

So in this chapter I'm asking the question: why do you think? Is it because a mind created the world, and therefore created things with minds as well? Or is it because in the beginning there was only matter, and that matter has resulted in minds through gradual processes of development?

And I've thrown out three things that I think need explanation in the world as we see it. If we began with a mineral Mordor, and purely material processes are responsible for everything, then I think we need a good explanation for the increasing order in the world over the last four billion years, the beauty that has emerged from the primeval chaos, and the origin of information from a jumble of atoms and molecules.

But I think the fourth thing that needs an explanation is probably the most important one: Where did life come from?

★ ★ ★

This is a big question. Life as we know it requires proteins, and proteins are formed by combining twenty different amino acids in the right order. A simple protein might have 100 amino acids in a chain, which means that the likelihood of assembling a protein correctly by blind chance is around 1 in 10^{130}, or smaller than the odds of winning the lottery eighteen times in a row. And that's just one protein. When we remember that life as we know it requires hundreds of thousands of proteins, we quickly become amazed by the fact that we exist at all.

So what possible explanations are there? We can probably rule out blind chance as being too unlikely. We can also rule out natural selection, because natural selection only works on matter that is already alive. Once we've done that, we're left with two major alternatives. One: a mind is the only way that such an extraordinary and specific set of complex things could have happened together (and again, you don't have to call that mind 'god', although lots of people do). Or two: as Richard Dawkins argued in *The Blind Watchmaker*, the chances are dramatically increased because there is a process of cumulative 'selection' at work, which means that the development of a protein is nothing like as random as it first appears.

This is a fiddly idea to get your head round, so Dawkins uses the analogy of a group of monkeys trying to type out a phrase from *Hamlet*. On their own, and without any guidance, their chances of success are exceptionally low – just as, he admits, the chances of getting a complex molecule by chance are too low to be believable. But, he asks, what if each time they typed a letter, it was compared to the target phrase, and if the letter was correct, the monkey could move on to the next letter? Suddenly, something that would otherwise take the monkey millions of years could be reduced to a few dozen attempts. The introduction of the target phrase, and the comparison between it and what the monkey is typing, combine to turn something very improbable into something quite achievable. Perhaps, he suggests, that's how we can account for the origin of life.

It's an intriguing idea, and when I first came across it, it sounded quite convincing. But look at the analogy for a minute. In order to explain how the origin of life could have happened without a divine mind, Dawkins has had to introduce two things – a target phrase, and a comparison with the monkey's typing – that have no equivalent in the entirely material, mindless mineral Mordor on which life is believed to have emerged 3.8 billion years ago. Even more surprisingly, he has brought in two things that clearly point to a mind being behind the origin of life: a pre-agreed goal (from where?), and an editing process in which progress towards that goal is monitored (by whom?).

I reckon, if you push it to the extreme, his analogy suggests that somebody (the head monkey? Shakespeare? God?) built the goal of life into the fabric of the earth when it began, and that the same somebody ensured that the goal was reached. Which sounds remarkably similar to the views of many religious people.

So I'm not sure that the target phrase approach shows anything much. Except, I guess, the difficulty of explaining the origin of life without a mind of some sort.

* * *

I hate sounding like a broken record, but I'll say it again: none of this proves that there is a god. And it certainly doesn't tell us much about what he/she/it/they might be like. But for my money, it does give a number of pieces of evidence that need to be considered when asking the question: why do you think?

Generally, when left on their own, things decay and become less ordered, but that doesn't seem to have happened on planet earth in the last few billion years. Instead, a planet that seems to have started as formless and void, which is an ancient way of saying 'an unsorted, lifeless mess', has become ordered, beautiful, and bursting with life. Douglas Adams was right about that – our planet is just like a beautiful garden – and I think that needs an explanation.

Generally, when left on their own, inanimate objects and chemicals don't generate information, and they don't initiate languages by which complex molecules can leave instructions for chemical factories, or develop 3.5 billion-letter blueprints that Bill Gates could describe as 'far, far more advanced than any software we've ever created'. Instead, when we see information, languages and codes in our world, we conclude that an intelligent mind is behind them (and the more complex the code, the more intelligent the mind).

Generally, when left on their own, clusters of minerals don't form enormously complicated combinations of proteins that gather into living cells and begin self-replicating. So, if biochemistry suggests that this happened, I think you could be forgiven for thinking, once again, that there's a mind at work.

That doesn't mean that none of these things could have happened without a mind, or a god. But I think it means that we can't use 'science' to rule out the possibility of a god. This is obvious in a way, because so many great scientists have believed in a god, yet the fact is lots of people talk like that, like it's 'God' or 'science', and you have to choose. But the way I see it, lots of events in our world have two causes: a physical cause ('I have a black eye because my cell tissue swelled up') and a personal cause ('I have a black eye because I stared at this guy's girlfriend'). Finding the first one doesn't mean that the second one doesn't exist.

I also think it means that if we're weighing up whether mind created matter, or matter created mind, we have a number of clues. I think the sorts of things we've been talking about in this chapter are clues that some mind, some creator, some sort of god, was responsible for the order, the beauty, the information and the life we see around us. If, on top of this, we throw into the mix the fact that our universe seems to be extremely finely tuned so that planets and living things can exist, we might well reckon that the possibility of God deserves some more consideration. We might even conclude it's the most likely explanation for all the scientific evidence we have.

If it was – hey, even if it *could* be – then we'd have to be prepared for anything. Ultimately, we might even have to reconsider what is possible in the first place.

5.
WHITE RAIN:
WHAT IS POSSIBLE?

Every British guy in his thirties has a mate called Dave. I don't know where they all come from, but it's just the way things are; even people called Dave have a mate called Dave. If you ring someone's mobile in the evening and they aren't there, it will usually be because they were out with their mate Dave, who is likely to have a nickname that rhymes, like 'Dave the save' or 'Dave the rave', or even 'Dave the knave' (although I haven't worked out why this is – not many of us have friends called 'Tony the pony' or 'Pete the sheet'). Your mate Dave is usually the guy you go for a drink with and talk to about things that matter. In practice, that means you often end up arguing with him, but you always remember that you like him anyway by the time you've finished.

I'm no exception. I'm in my thirties, I have a mate called Dave, and we often end up talking about important stuff, and disagreeing about it. There's one question, though, that me and Dave disagree about more than any other, and it's this: What is possible? Dave is convinced that we can know the limits of what's possible, and that there's no such thing as a 'miracle' or a 'supernatural event' (whatever these are). When he was growing up, he came across quite a few people who believed in superstitious nonsense, and quite a few people who used the word 'miracle' all the time, even when it referred to things that could easily be explained within the laws of nature, and people like this, Dave says, undermine reason and particularly science. Plus, he doesn't believe in a God who is involved with the world, and he definitely doesn't believe in angels or spirits or anything like that. So he's very sceptical of anything 'supernatural'. So as far as Dave's concerned, anything that breaks 'the laws of nature' can't have happened. He's completely convinced about that.

I'm not so sure, though. I mean, I often find myself agreeing with him, and laughing, when he tells me about some of the crazy stuff he's heard. At times, I've chucked in a few stories of my own (like the Hindu milk-drinking god, and the Catholic pilgrims in Portugal in 1917 who claimed that the sun rushed dramatically towards the earth as part of an appearance of the Virgin Mary). I also find the number of British people who believe the stars influence their future very bizarre, and I love Dave's passion for reason and science – I'd rather have him write our textbooks than almost anyone else I know. But I'm still unsettled by his unshakeable confidence that we know nothing 'supernatural' can ever happen. Underneath it all, I'm not sure he's thought it all through.

For a start, the fact that a lot of oddballs believe something doesn't mean it isn't true. As I often remind him, a lot of cranks believe in the Welfare State, and care for the planet, and atheism, and most other things Dave believes in, but that doesn't mean those things aren't valid. I also think you have to be careful when saying that something never happens, particularly when it's something that lots of other people claim has happened to them. (A few years back, I remember seeing several polls about 'supernatural events', which all agreed that around 70% of people in the UK believed in them. Dave grinned, and said that just showed how silly 70% of people really are.) But to say something never happens is a very strong statement: you might say that it doesn't always happen, or that it doesn't normally happen, but to rule it out altogether means you need to know beyond reasonable doubt that it could never happen. And I don't think Dave can know that.

But I think Dave's biggest problem is this: his certainty that supernatural events don't exist is grounded in his certainty that *God* doesn't exist. We talked about that once, and he admitted it.

'Yeah, you're right. If I believed in a god, I might believe in miracles, but I don't, so I don't. But the Pope's got the same problem. He only believes in miracles because he believes in God.'

'Maybe.'

'No, definitely. If he didn't believe in God, he wouldn't believe in miracles either, would he?'

'Probably not.'

'In fact,' Dave said, sounding rather more confident, 'the Pope's worse than me. The Pope believes in God because he believes in miracles, like the virgin birth and stuff – but he only believes in miracles because he believes in God. That's like using unicorns to prove your belief in mythical creatures, and then using mythical creatures to explain why you believe in unicorns. He's going round and round in circles.'

I thought about this.

'But,' I said tentatively, 'aren't you going round in circles as well?'

'No, not really.'

'Yes, you are. Why don't you believe in a god?'

'Because there's no evidence for it. In my world, you need evidence to believe in something, not to disbelieve in something,' he said, eyebrows raised innocently.

'Right, but what would you say if the Pope said that the virgin birth was evidence for God?'

'I'd say it didn't constitute evidence for anything, because it never happened. It's a myth. Just a very widely believed one.' Dave loves saying things like that.

'You may be right, but how can you be so sure?'

'Because supernatural events don't happen.'

'But you just said that they might, if there was a god.'

There was a pause, as Dave reflected on the implications of this.

'Well maybe me and the Pope are both arguing in circles. But if that proves anything, it just proves that miracles can't be used as evidence one way or the other.'

'Well, perhaps.'

We left it there. But over time – don't you hate it when you finish an argument, and then think of all the things you should have said? – I began to think that there was a huge flaw in Dave's thinking, and in mine. What I realized was, there should have been a third category of person in that conversation, not just Dave and the Pope.

Dave's view goes: God definitely doesn't exist → 'miracles' certainly don't happen → there's no need to consider evidence for them.

The Pope's view, for all I know, might run: God definitely exists → 'miracles' certainly happen → there's no particular need to investigate them.

But what if your belief system, like that of lots of people in this country, was in between the two? I think it's perfectly possible to believe: God may or may not exist → 'miracles' may or may not happen → 'miracles' should be investigated, to see whether or not there's any evidence for them.

All of which means, if God is possible – and I've talked a fair bit already about why I think he is – then he could theoretically do whatever he wanted, couldn't he? I would think, if there were a Creator God, he could make virgins give birth, or dead people rise, or blind people see, or make green skies, or white rain, or anything else he chose. That's not to say we'd believe every account of something like that happening (and actually, I think there are very good reasons not to believe in an awful lot of accounts, because there's so much gullibility, deception and fraud around). But the bottom line is, if God is possible, then supernatural events are possible, too, aren't they? So I don't think we can rule them out altogether. We just need to investigate them like we'd investigate anything else, comparing different explanations – and if a supernatural event fits the evidence better than the alternatives, then so be it.

★ ★ ★

To be fair, a lot of clever people disagree with me about this. In fact, some clever people are so sure that 'miracles' are impossible that they don't give them a moment's thought, often quoting a Scottish philosopher called David Hume to explain why. When I was at university, people often did this in conversation, and I've since come across it in several of the fashionable best-sellers written in the last few years about how everyone who believes in God is an ignorant nutcase who wants to blow up buildings, teach fairy tales to your children, take over the government and throw rotten fruit at gay people. (For the record, the religious people I know aren't generally like this, though I realize that doesn't mean there aren't any.) So it's worth thinking for a minute about how David Hume argued, and whether what he said was true:

> A miracle is a violation of the laws of nature; and as a firm and
> unalterable experience has established these laws, the proof

against a miracle, from the very nature of the fact, is as entire as any argument from experience as can be imagined . . .

It is no miracle that a man, seemingly in good health, should die on a sudden: because such a kind of death, though more unusual than any other, has yet been frequently observed to happen. But it is a miracle that a dead man should come to life; because that has never been observed, in any age or country. There must, therefore, be a uniform experience against every miraculous event, otherwise the event would not merit that appellation.

I think there are a couple of things Hume says here that just don't quite work. The first is his definition of what a 'miracle' actually is (which is why I keep using the word in quotation marks – I think his definition and mine might be different). In the last sentence above, he says that an event would not be called 'miraculous' unless there was a 'uniform experience' against it, which is effectively defining a 'miracle' as 'something that has never happened in human experience'. Of course, if you define it like that, all you're saying is: things that never happen, never happen. Which is obvious, but not very helpful.

Then there's the bit when he says that a dead man coming to life 'has never been observed, in any age or country'. To be honest, I'm not quite sure what this means. It either means: 'No human being has ever claimed to have seen someone die, and then live again', in which case, isn't he simply ignoring all sorts of people who claim to have seen exactly that? Or it might mean: 'Yes, human beings have claimed to see dead people who are alive again, but they were all wrong', which I think must be what he meant. But how does he know this? I'm not quite sure, but my guess is, he's only saying it because he believes that miracles never happen. In fact, it sounds to me like he's arguing in a circle, just like Dave (and maybe the

Pope): miracles are never observed, so they don't happen, so if people think they've seen miracles they're wrong, so miracles are never observed. It sounds like he's putting any reports of 'miracles', no matter what the evidence, in a bit of a catch-22 situation. So I'm not convinced it's a very good argument.

Here's how I've thought about it. Taking our 70% of people who believe in supernatural events of some kind (that's a Western figure, and I'd be willing to bet it's a fair bit higher in most of Africa, Asia and South America), let's say that only one in ten of those people have ever actually witnessed what they called a 'miracle', and the others only believe in them because of hearsay. That would still mean that 7% of people, and probably even more globally, had witnessed something they believed was a supernatural event – a group that would number in the hundreds of millions worldwide. So I don't think David Hume, and all those who have followed him, can sweep miracles under the carpet as 'never observed' because of 'firm and unalterable experience'. If I can be a bit harsh for a moment, it sounds to me like he's just ignoring the evidence.

I'm also bothered by his understanding of what the 'laws of nature' actually are. He thinks that having laws of nature means that nobody, not even the creator of those laws (if he exists), can interrupt them. Ever. But let's say, for a moment, that there was a Creator God who had made the universe, and established regular laws of physics and chemistry. Let's say that these laws governed the universe the whole time, except when the Creator himself decided to break them – and then let's say that the Creator decided to do so, for his own reasons, to bring people back to life, open blind eyes, or whatever else. Why would this be impossible?

My little sister used to love playing with the slinky. She would set it going at the top of the stairs, and watch, fascinated, as all by itself it would descend from stair to stair, moving entirely by gravity and the springs within it. But from time to time, she would intervene in its natural journey when it was halfway down the stairs, moving it down two stairs at once, or sending it back up a few. When she did this, she wasn't undoing the natural laws of how slinkies work; she was just an intelligent being, coming in from outside the system she had designed, to adjust it as she wanted to.

It's a silly illustration, I know, but you get the point. Hume's argument is very convincing if we can be sure there is no god, or if we can be sure that no god would ever intervene with the slinky for any reason. But what if we can't? What if the existence of God were possible, or even probable – what then?

* * *

Call me crazy, but if there's a god, I think it's a bit of a stretch to tell him what he can and can't do. If we're talking about the Creator of the cosmos, the sustainer of the stars with the whole world in his hands, then I'm not convinced we can turn around and say, *that's not what normally happens, so you can't do that.* That's just not the sort of thing you say to someone who builds galaxies. And I'm sure we can't say, *that's not what I would do, so I can be certain that you wouldn't.* So if there's a god – and I know that's a big if, but we've talked about that – then I think we should get out of the habit of saying that things are impossible. To be honest, I wouldn't have thought that would be very controversial.

It probably isn't, in most places. Most builders' yards, and coffee shops, and playgroups are filled with people who know that, if God exists, he can do whatever he likes. The main places where people don't realize this are universities. I read a lot of religious literature at university, and I was often surprised at the confidence of academics that God couldn't do this or wouldn't do that. Which would be fine if they were all atheists, and didn't believe in God anyway; but most of them weren't, yet they still wrote lengthy books on the basis that things like making sick people better, or knowing what would happen next, or making it rain lots, were impossible for God – even though, many of them believed, that same God created the Ring Galaxy, and around 100 billion others. I used to sit there in libraries and lecture halls, thinking, *but if the God these guys are writing about is real, and the universe is as big as we think it is, then raising dead people or making it rain lots aren't hard, are they? They're not even close. So what's the problem?*

* * *

I sometimes wonder whether people don't believe in 'miracles' because they know that, if they do, they might have to believe in God as well. When I was at university, I remember a three-o'clock-in-the-morning discussion with my friend Greg, whom we met earlier, who is one of the cleverest guys I know. That morning, I'd heard someone I knew explain that they'd been instantly healed of a sickness when someone else had prayed for them. So I told the story to Greg, because I wanted to know how he would respond. I'll never forget what he said, because it showed me just how much is at stake in this whole discussion. 'If I believed what you've just told me,' he said carefully and graciously, 'the entire way I look at the physical world would have to change.'

He was right. It would.

* * *

When you've been reading British newspapers for a while, you get to know some absolutely unbreakable rules. Some of them are obvious and political: the *Mirror* will always support Labour; the *Daily Express* will always support the Tories; and the *Sun* will always support whoever is likely to win the next election. Other rules are to do with ideology: whenever there's a financial wobble, the left-wing papers will say it's because the markets are too free, and *The Economist* will say it's because they're not free enough. Others are to do with style: William Rees-Mogg will always say exactly what you thought he would say, and Julie Birchill will always say exactly the opposite of what you thought she would say. But above all of these, there is one rule that is even more unbreakable than the others. If the government has spent any money unnecessarily, the *Daily Mail* will find out about it.

On Tuesday 11 December 2007, under the headline 'We don't do miracles', the *Mail* ran an extraordinary story on page 5 about a woman called June Clarke. 'Power of prayer helps woman to walk again,' declared the subtitle incredulously, 'yet officials refuse to stop her benefits.' Mrs Clarke, a fifty-six-year-old from Plymouth, had slipped on a wet floor at work in 2000, and had ended up damaging her spine, with the result that she spent the next six years in a wheelchair. But at a Christian conference in January 2006, the *Mail* reported, she was physically healed, and within hours had folded up her wheelchair and stopped taking painkillers. After four months, having seen her doctor and realized that she was permanently cured, Mrs Clarke contacted the government's industrial injury department, to tell them the good news that they no longer needed to pay her any benefits, because God had miraculously healed her. So far, so good.

If that had been the end of the story, I doubt it would have made the papers. Personally, I've seen things like that happen dozens of times, but none of them makes their way into the national news. What made Mrs Clarke's case different, and what attracted the outrage of the *Mail* and later the BBC, was the reaction of the government department, who in a moment of inspired bureaucracy refused to stop her incapacity benefits because, 'We haven't got a button to push that says "miracle".' (You couldn't make this stuff up.)

You see, because of the permanent nature of her injury, she had been put on incapacity benefits for life, which meant the computer system at the benefits office was completely unable to cope with her miraculous healing, and she continued to receive payments that she felt she didn't deserve. You can just imagine it, some poor guy sitting in an office in Basingstoke, rummaging around the database to see if 'miracle' is on their system, which it isn't, and then contacting his supervisor, who also has no idea what to do about Mrs Clarke and her mysterious empty wheelchair, and tells him to get off the phone. Eventually, Mrs Clarke went to consult a government doctor, who declared her fully fit, and her payments were finally stopped. She has since been able to repay her debt by working full-time as a carer.

I sometimes wonder how David Hume would respond to a story like that. Sadly, we'll never know. From what I know of him, he probably wouldn't have been a *Mail* reader anyway.

* * *

When I talk to people who don't believe supernatural events are possible, they usually talk about it in one of two ways.

Some people say that modern science has proved they're impossible, which is a bit weird, because I don't think eighteenth-century white guys were the first people to discover that blind people couldn't suddenly see, or that dead people didn't come back to life again. The way I view it, science can tell you how the laws of nature work, and make very accurate predictions about what will happen next (except when it comes to the weather), but it can't guarantee you that there is no God, no Creator, no intelligent being who can heal or raise people from the dead if he wants to. That's just not what science is. It can tell you what the *slinky* will do next, but it can't tell you what *my sister* will do next. If she exists.

The other thing people say is that even if there was a God who could do 'miracles', he wouldn't. Why, they wonder, would God make laws of nature, only to break them? Why would he heal some people and not others? I remember being on a radio show once, talking about this, and the other guy in the studio said, 'Even assuming that there is a god, I don't think he would behave in that way. For example, if he could make a blind man see, why doesn't he make all blind men see?'

When he said that, I thought, *Yes, but how do we know what God would do? You can't prove someone can't do something, just because you can't think of a reason why they haven't done it.* If we're talking about the Creator of the universe, which that guy in the studio was doing, it seems strange to be so certain of what he would and wouldn't do. And it seems very strange to say that God can't have healed Mrs Clarke because he didn't also heal Mrs Jones, and we think he should have done. Where did we get that from?

Let's say I take my children to the seaside, and I take a walk with my son Zeke and buy him an ice-cream. If Zeke goes back and tells the others he got one, they might well feel upset that I didn't get one for all of them, which would be understandable. But I don't think they'd conclude that, since I am a good father and I love them all equally, I can't have bought Zeke an ice-cream in the first place.

And it would be really odd if some random man saw me at the ice-cream van, and then went off to tell his friends that buying my son an ice-cream was impossible – because if I'd bought one for Zeke, I should have bought one for the entire beach. I mean, that would be completely bizarre. Most people on the beach didn't know me, or care that I was there, and almost none of them was even asking for an ice-cream, so surely it's OK for me not to buy them one?

Now I know that walking out of a wheelchair isn't an ice-cream, and I know that I'm not God. Illustrations always break down somewhere. My point is: it's fine to say we'd like God to heal everybody. But I doubt we can say that if he doesn't, he's not allowed to heal anybody.

* * *

So what is possible?

Well, if there is no God, then only things that conform to scientific laws are possible (unless you believe in an infinite number of universes, in which case everything must be possible somewhere – but that idea is so weird that I can't really get my head round it, because it means there must be at least one in which Shakespeare is a nude bungee jumper and Alan Partridge is President).

But if there is a God, or if there might well be, then pretty much anything is possible. I don't think you'd get logical impossibilities – so no, you wouldn't get the famous rock so big you can't lift it – but you could quite easily have blind people seeing, or white rain, or people being raised from the dead.

Of course, to say that something is possible doesn't necessarily mean it's probable. It's really important to say this, because otherwise the whole discussion becomes a bit all-or-nothing: either we have no miracles, ever, because they're impossible; or we have a world in which Hindu statues drink milk, and wide-eyed cloth-wearing cranks can see into the future, and the sun is free to rush towards Portugal (miracle!), and all the while nobody else on earth notices (another miracle!). We can't have that. The fact that supernatural events are possible doesn't mean that they're always likely.

In fact, I think we work out whether supernatural events have happened in exactly the same way as we work out anything else. We look at the evidence; we consider what alternative explanations there are; and we choose which one fits the data more simply, and more coherently, than the others. Personally, I find it easier to believe that a handful of Roman Catholic pilgrims got a bit over-excited while staring at the sun (which can't be good for you), than that the earth leapt out of its orbit and flew across the solar system without it being noticed by anyone outside of Portugal. On the other hand, when faced with several independent witnesses of something, and normally sceptical sources (the BBC and the *Mail*, for instance) reporting it as fact, and no other credible explanation presenting itself, then I might conclude that a supernatural event was the best way of explaining an empty wheelchair.

Or even an empty tomb, for that matter.

INTERVAL. THE RIPPING OF MR PRITCHARD: WHERE ARE WE SO FAR?

We're halfway through the book now, so it might be a good time to review where we've come so far, and where we're going next.

In chapter 1, I shared my experiences of fundamentalism, and explained how and why I'd concluded that we all need evidence for what we believe. The second chapter was all about what evidence looks like: how we know anything, how we decide between competing explanations, and what we can do if the thing we're considering can't be proven mathematically or scientifically, like most human knowledge can't be. In some ways, the first two chapters were really common-sense chapters, but I thought I'd write them anyway because it took me so long to realize them myself (and because so many people I know still struggle with either or both of them).

Chapters 3 and 4 were mostly about science. The big idea was that the physical world around us gives some important clues about whether or not there is a god – the fine-tuning of the physical constants in the universe (chapter 3), and the transformation of a formless, informationless, lifeless mess into a world filled with beauty, data, DNA and all kinds of life (chapter 4). I said that these things don't prove there's a God, and they certainly don't tell us what he's like, but they do provide clues that a mind of some sort, a Creator God with intelligence and power, might be behind it all.

Then just now, I was talking about how the possibility of God opens the door to the possibility of supernatural events. Again, some of this might have seemed obvious, but I know lots of writers and thinkers for whom it is far from obvious, and quite a few who think you can prove the opposite. So I wanted to explain why I think that link – from 'God is possible' to 'miracles are possible' – makes sense. That's a basic overview of where we've travelled so far.

Looked at another way, what I've written is an explanation of why several popular worldviews around today, at least in Britain, don't quite work for me. These would include fundamentalism (chapter 1), phenomenalism and positivism (chapter 2), atheism and materialism (chapters 3 and 4) and deism (chapter 5). It's not that I've somehow proved they're impossible, but hopefully I've explained why I just find them hard to believe in the light of the evidence we have. The one major type of worldview that's left, and which I'll talk about more in the second half of the book, is theism: the belief in a God.

★ ★ ★

I think it's fair enough to try to use physics, biology and chemistry to establish whether we believe there is a God or not. I've tried to do it myself. But if we want to get any further than that – if we want to know what he/she/it/they might be like, and whether they have done or said anything, and why the world is as it is, and what that might mean for our lives – then we need to unleash the arts. Science is incredibly useful for all sorts of things, including the stuff we've talked about already, but if we're talking about ultimate meaning and personality and story and destiny, I don't think we should be limited to things that can be expressed using laboratory equipment or formulae (which is the impression I sometimes get from reading angry people who denounce religion – although, to be fair, these people are very rarely professional scientists). We also need to get into the study of things like history, society, literature and theology.

I mean, if you want to understand a light wave, or a cancer, you need the sciences. If you're in hospital with a physical sickness, you want men and women of science to sort you out, and you're unlikely to be in the mood for a ditty on the trials of the human condition. But if you want to understand a poem, or a piece of music, or the experience of falling in love, you need the arts. Science may be able to help with the mechanics of these things (ink, sound waves, hormones or whatever), but it is art that unlocks the meaning they hold, the hope they express, the stories they evoke. And it occurs to me that understanding God (if he exists) and his dealings with human beings (if there have been any) would probably be more like understanding poetry, or music or love, than understanding a light wave or a cancer.

You can get too scientific with things like art, beauty, literature and theology, and if you do, you can end up in a real mess. For example, some people say that our passion for beauty is just because of evolution, so we only find landscapes beautiful because our ancestors could find food there. When I hear that, I often think, *but the most beautiful things I've seen, like the Himalayas or the Grand Canyon, don't have much food in them these days, and I doubt they ever did. And I don't care how much food you can find there, out-of-town shopping malls with burger vans and Pizza Huts are never going to seem beautiful to anybody.* Do you see what I mean? No matter how hard we are pushed, most of us struggle to believe that our desires to write poems and paint canvasses and worship God are *entirely* about spreading our genes. It's like science can take us so far, but no further.

There's a great scene in the movie *Dead Poets Society*, where Robin Williams, an inspirational young English teacher in a stuffy old boarding school, gets his class to read an essay by J. Evans Pritchard called 'Understanding Poetry'. A dutiful student reads the essay aloud, which explains how to work out a poem's greatness scientifically by drawing a graph, scoring it on perfection and importance, and multiplying them together for the total greatness of the poem. As the student completes his reading, the bored class wait for Robin Williams to begin his analysis.

'Excrement!' he pronounces deliberately, and a number of the class look up in shock. 'That's what I think of Mr. J. Evans Pritchard! We're not laying pipe, we're talking about poetry. I mean, how can you describe poetry like American Bandstand: "I like Byron, I give him a 42, but I can't dance to it"? Now I want you to rip out that page. Go on, rip out the entire page.'

By now, many in the class are looking at him as if he has gone mad. Undaunted, he continues his rant, urging the class to join in, and one by one the students begin the ripping of Mr Pritchard.

'Gentlemen, tell you what, don't just tear out that page, tear out the entire introduction. I want it gone, history. Leave nothing of it. Rip it out. Rip! Begone, J. Evans Pritchard, PhD! Rip, shred, tear! Rip it out! I want to hear nothing but ripping of Mr. Pritchard. We'll perforate it, put it on a roll . . . Armies of academics going forward, measuring poetry. No! We'll not have that here.'

And so begins the movie's central plot, as Robin Williams attempts to liberate the boys in his class from the passionless, unimaginative, technical approach to learning that the entire school seems to be ensnared in. The scene made a profound impact on me when I first watched it: scientific analysis is essential for engineering and medicine, but it is totally inappropriate to make it the primary tool for engaging with poetry, or music, or love. It may have taken over the school, and even the academy, for now, but anyone with a soul can see that poetry will not be chained by it, nor should it be.

I think the same is true of theology. It's quite common these days to find people saying that theology isn't a proper subject because it's not scientific, or (worse) that God is a scientific hypothesis and should be treated as such (what kind of experiments would that produce, I wonder?). The former Russian president, Nikita Khrushchev, famously said that cosmonaut Yuri Gagarin had flown into space, but 'hadn't seen any God there' – which, as one academic responded, is a bit like saying that Hamlet had been into his attic and hadn't found Shakespeare. I think people who argue this sort of thing need to experience something of the ripping of Mr Pritchard.

★ ★ ★

So in the second half of this book, we will move on to the arts: stories, sociology and literature (chapters 6 and 7), history (chapter 8), and theology (chapter 9). We'll look at some of the basic questions that human beings live with, and how they might overlap with some of the big stories that we have been telling for thousands of years.

I want to start by asking a question that is pretty foundational to everyone on planet earth: What's wrong with the world?

6.
A HORNET IN THE ICING: WHAT'S WRONG WITH THE WORLD?

If you ever have a bit of spare time and want to start an interesting conversation with a stranger, I recommend the question: 'What's wrong with the world?' I doubt there's anyone on earth who doesn't have an opinion on it. You'll be amazed. You just go to your nearest shopping centre, tell people you're doing a survey and would value their opinion, and then ask them what's wrong with the world – before you know it, you'll be talking through some of their most foundational beliefs, and they'll be sharing thoughts that only their partner and their pets have ever heard before. Just two tips: don't wear a uniform, and don't carry a clipboard. People in shopping centres are very good at avoiding you if you've got a bib and a clipboard.

I've asked several hundred people what's wrong with the world in the last few years, sometimes individually and sometimes in groups, and there are basically three types of answer. The first one is the 'problems-at-the-moment' answer. You can always tell that one because it's been in the newspapers that month, so people say things like 'immigration' or 'bankers' or some other topic which you know is just a current-affairs answer, because if you'd asked them a year ago they'd have said something else. When they do this, I sometimes try to clarify: 'So you're saying that if there were no bankers, or no immigration, the world would be free from problems?' Most people will get what I mean at this point, and maybe give it a bit more thought. But if they still insist that bankers, or immigration, are the main things wrong with the world, I don't worry about it; the chances are that either they are very stubborn, or they live in the woods and haven't washed for a while.

The second one is the 'problems-with-the-world' answer. Things like cancer. Earthquakes. AIDS. Global warming, disease, tsunamis, volcanoes, miscarriages, famine, babies dying, flooding. Nobody mentions all of these: the ones they pick depend on what's happened recently, and on their personal experience. If you talk to enough people, though, these subjects all come up.

The third and final type is 'problems with bad people'. War. Religious fanaticism. Genocide, torture, terrorism, paedophilia, drug abuse, murder, rape. Injustice. I'm not saying anyone will call these things 'problems with bad people', because they probably won't; most of us think about them in the abstract, as if there is a thing out there called 'War' that needs to be found, arrested and executed. (Come to think of it, why not? We've declared war on other abstract nouns, like 'terror', so why not a 'war on War'?) But when you get under the skin of it, all of these awful things are simply human beings doing terrible things to other human beings. People may give some smaller-scale examples, like bullying or drink-driving, but in essence they are all saying that what's wrong with the world is other people doing bad things.

Don't take my word for it. Just leave your bib and your clipboard at home, and go for a walk round the shops this afternoon, asking people. You might get the occasional curveball – what's wrong with the world is gnomes, or aliens or my next-door neighbour – but in general, my guess is you'll find that people's answers fit in one of those three categories. And I think that's very interesting.

It's interesting because nobody ever says 'nothing'. The fact that we don't live in a perfect world is almost a proverb in our culture. I mean, you could be sitting on a Tuscan hilltop, staring in wonder as cypress trees and rustic church bell-towers for miles around are gently illuminated by the warm, yellow evening light, as the clouds play kiss chase across the sky and their mottled shadows dance across the vineyards, your glass of Barolo in hand, listening to Louis Armstrong sing 'What a Wonderful World', and I still doubt you'd be able to look another human being in the eye and tell them nothing was wrong with the world. No matter who we are or what our experience is, we all seem to accept that something isn't quite right.

Yet this world is all we've ever known. None of us has ever known a world without disease, or suffering, or war or injustice. So it's surprising how certain we are that something is wrong with it. As one Oxford don famously put it, it's like a fish being continually surprised at the wetness of water. Where does this sense of something being *wrong* with the world come from? What are we comparing our world to?

A few months back, Rachel was looking after our three-year-old nephew Charlie, and they were watching *The Life of Mammals* by David Attenborough. She became concerned when the commentary and images began depicting lions getting ready for a night hunt, and she realized that Charlie was about to witness some savage, blood-and-guts footage of a beautiful and elegant zebra (basically a stripy horsey, of course) being torn to pieces by a pack of lions. But Charlie was transfixed by the early stages of the chase, his eyes as wide as saucers, and so Rachel had no choice but to let the sequence run its course. It was every bit as gruesome as she had feared. The zebra was in full sprint when one of the pride leaped through the air, dug its claws into her back, and sank its jaws into her hindquarters, ripping flesh across the screen and causing the zebra to jerk backwards and collapse in a pathetic heap, before being devoured by the rest of the pride.

Rachel waited for the inevitable shrieks, tears and hysteria from Charlie. But instead, there was a short pause, a brief sideways glance, and then a single word, delivered as only a three-year-old can. 'Uh-oh,' he said, philosophically. And with that, he turned his eyes back to the screen to watch the cheetahs.

Three-year-olds know that cute things don't always prevail, that even friendly animals die, and that the strong kill the weak. That's just the way the world works, and there's nothing particularly wrong with it; it may be worth a resigned 'uh-oh', but not much more. So why isn't it the same when human beings suffer? Why is it, when we see television reports of the devastation caused by earthquakes, or read about what a paedophile has done to his victims, or reflect on the horrors of the Rwandan genocide or the Holocaust, that we don't simply turn to one another, shrug our shoulders, and say, 'uh-oh'? After all, everyone dies, the strong kill the weak, and they always have done. So what's wrong with that?

But of course we all know there's a lot wrong with that. Animals killing weaker animals so they can eat, or control territory, or have more offspring, is normal; humans killing weaker humans so they can do those things is unspeakably appalling, and causes a visceral, gut-wrenching reaction in all of us when we read about it.

Last night I was watching a documentary called *Mugabe and the White African*, about the forced eviction of farmers from land in Zimbabwe, and one in particular who stood his ground and won a landmark case against the regime in an international court. At one point in the film, the three main characters were assaulted and badly beaten up by a group of land raiders, and the images of their faces immediately afterwards made me feel quite sick. *How can anyone do that to other people, just for a piece of land?*, I thought. But the weird thing is, animals do it all the time. They fight each other for land, and the one with the bigger horns, or the sharper teeth, gets the land, and the weaker one gets a beating.

So what is it that makes us watch this happen to animals with an unperturbed fascination, while we recoil in horror when it happens to humans – not just because we don't particularly like it, but because we have a strong sense that it is wrong, unjust, evil? Where does that sense of right and wrong, so alien in the animal kingdom, actually come from?

★ ★ ★

There's another interesting thing about the answers people give to the question: 'What's wrong with the world?' If you strip out the 'problems-at-the-moment' answer, which is usually a bit of a knee-jerk response anyway, then the two problems you're left with are very religious in nature: death and sin. Which, in a world that professes no longer to be scared of the first, nor to believe in the second, is a bit of a shock.

To be fair, lots of people don't say 'death' when you ask them. It's not a word we generally like using, unless it's followed by words that soften it a bit, like 'of a salesman' or 'by chocolate'. But I think that's what they mean when they say things like earthquakes, volcanoes, cancer, AIDS, flooding and so on. They mean that lots of things in the natural world cause death to human beings, and that is a huge problem.

The way I know this is that nobody objects to earthquakes if they don't kill anyone. If there's a mild tremor that shakes the crockery, it's faintly exciting; sometimes, really big earthquakes can happen, but because they take place in the middle of the ocean somewhere and nobody dies, we never hear about them. A few years ago a volcano in Iceland erupted, and flights across Europe were grounded for days because of the ash cloud – but because nobody died as a direct result, you had all sorts of odd features on the news about how good it was for the environment that all those planes had stopped flying for a few days. (There's something quite odd about a situation where the best part of a mountain is floating around in the sky somewhere, and people still think it's good for air quality.) Again, I'm not sure that any disease, whether cancer, AIDS, or anything else, would be held responsible for the world's problems if people didn't die from it. So it seems that, when people reply with the 'problems-with-the-world' answer, what they're really pointing the finger at is death.

Similarly, when people mention things like torture, genocide, rape, terrorism and so on, they are talking about what theologians call 'sin', even if they use words like 'evil' or 'injustice' instead (which they generally do – I guess the word 'sin' sounds a bit small to modern ears, as if it's really about one drink too many, or a parking ticket, rather than mass murder or paedophilia or whatever). But they're saying that what's wrong with the world is that people do awful things to one another. So, presumably, if we could get rid of the compulsion in some people to do bad things, we could solve the world's problems.

★ ★ ★

Having said that, working out who's bad and who's not is more difficult than you'd think. Unless you read the tabloid newspapers, of course, which trumpet the 'bad-apple' theory on a weekly basis: there are a few bad apples out there, but they shouldn't make us concerned about the rest of the barrel. (Usually this takes the form of a sinister mugshot of an unshaven, stocky, scowling man, with a caption that runs: 'Look! A Bad Man who does Bad Things! Lucky the rest of us aren't like that!' Or words to that effect.) But I think that's hopelessly naïve, and it doesn't even begin to engage with how human evil works.

I've caused a huge amount of suffering. I've never killed or raped anyone, but over a lifetime of selfish, arrogant, manipulative stupidity, I've left a trail of crushed and damaged people in my wake. Most of the time I haven't even stayed long enough to see the wounds, or the tears, but occasionally you see the pain in someone's face, and you realize that, to that person, you're just Hitler without the moustache. I'm sure there are people scattered around Britain today who still bear deep emotional scars because of things I've said or done, and I wouldn't be surprised if some of the guys at my boarding school, or some of the girls I knew at university, would travel across the country to spit on my corpse. For those people, getting rid of suffering in the world would mean getting rid of *me*.

I got an email a few months back from another writer, and he put it like this. Imagine I'm trying to rid the world of suffering, and I decide to wipe out the very worst people in history: Hitler, Pol Pot, Mao, Stalin, whoever. That would mean that the worst people left in the world were the next tier of evil: serial killers, rapists, child molesters. So I chuck them out next. In a world without those people, the most evil people on earth might be the thieves and the drink-drivers, maybe swindlers, cheats, liars, adulterers, who knows? So I have to wipe them out too. Before long, I'll be forced to discover the shocking reality that *I am now the worst person in the world*. Yet the world still isn't rid of suffering, because I cause so much suffering myself – I bully, manipulate, drive too fast, hurt people, say bad things, think worse things . . . In that world, I am a byword for evil, a pop-culture reference point for all-consuming villainy. In that world, I am Hitler.

So I don't think the line between good and evil runs between 'me' and 'the other', however convenient it might be to believe that. Both good and evil live together, and fight it out on a daily basis, in my own soul.

★ ★ ★

That's what Aleksandr Solzhenitsyn thought, and he ought to know. I doubt there are many people in the last century more qualified to talk about evil.

Solzhenitsyn was a Red Army captain in the Second World War, and he was arrested in February 1945 for making negative comments about Stalin in a letter to a friend. He was interrogated and beaten in Moscow, and then sentenced to eight years in a forced labour camp, followed by exile in southern Kazakhstan. Released by Khrushchev in 1956, he published *One Day in the Life of Ivan Denisovich*, which brought the prison labour system to light in the West, followed by his seminal *The Gulag Archipelago*, for which he was arrested again by the KGB in 1974, deported, and stripped of his Soviet citizenship. Despite his persecutions inside the Soviet Union, he was recognized as a genius outside it, and he was awarded the Nobel Prize for Literature in 1970.

It's not very often that brilliant writers encounter so many of the world's great evils first-hand – the Second World War, torture, the Gulag, and so on – so it's worth listening to him when he says what's wrong with the world. He makes uncomfortable reading, though. We want him to say that there are some really evil people, like Stalin, and they make life hell for the rest of us. But he doesn't let us off the hook that easily. Instead, he critiques communism and capitalism alike, which bothers those of us who think one is all bad and the other is all good. Then he compares himself to his captors in the Gulag, reminding us of some of the things he did during the war, and asking if he was really any better than they were. Finally, he argues that the problem of evil is not fundamentally communist, or totalitarian, or capitalist, but human: 'If only there were evil people somewhere insidiously committing evil deeds, and it were necessary only to separate them from the rest of us and destroy them.' (In other words, I'd love it if the 'bad-apple' theory was true.) 'But,' he continues, *the line dividing good and evil cuts through the heart of every human being*. And who is willing to destroy a piece of his own heart?'

* * *

Oddly, the most pithy statement of this idea comes from a letter that never was. It's often said that in 1910, *The Times* invited letters from its readers to answer the question: 'What's wrong with the world?', and the writer G. K. Chesterton responded with the shortest newspaper letter ever published:

> Dear Sir,
>   I am.
> Yours faithfully,
> G. K. Chesterton

I think that's just about the most profound thing that's ever been said about evil. Which makes it all the more weird that *The Times* never published such a letter (I checked with the archive), and nobody knows for sure how the rumour got started. Maybe Chesterton wrote it and it was never published.

Maybe he joked about it with a friend one day, in a sort of 'what-if?' conversation. Maybe someone just made it up, like 70% of your body heat escaping through your head, and chuckled to themselves as it got repeated everywhere, until even the American Chesterton Society thought it was true. Who knows? But wherever it got started, it's incredibly insightful. The problem with the world is that I'm in it, and if it wasn't me, it would be somebody else.

★ ★ ★

I'm not saying that this is the whole story. Besides causing huge suffering to one another, we are also obviously capable of astonishing creativity, compassion, invention and education. As we've developed over the last few thousand years, we've learned how to prolong life, increase material wealth and reduce physical pain, so in some strange ways we are both the cause of many of the world's problems and also the solution. I imagine that's why almost all our art forms express both tragedy and comedy, and why the most compelling ones combine the two. Tragedy and comedy, problem and solution, hope and despair, they're all jumbled up together in the human condition.

But despite developing in so many ways, I can't see that we've made any progress whatsoever in wiping out evil. The problems with our species, the deep character flaws that make us do the unpleasant things we do – I'm thinking of pride, insecurity, greed, stuff like that – have not gone away with the marching of time, and that means we still cause just as much suffering to one another as we always have done. (If anything, we actually cause more, because swords have been replaced by bombs, and people now spread vicious gossip to millions over the internet rather than to dozens in the village square.) I think that's significant. It suggests to me that, as well as being fundamentally creative, beautiful and intelligent, we as humans are also flawed, proud, insecure and greedy – not just for cultural reasons, or just in this century, but in the depths of our souls, from the Stone Age to the webpage, as part of the fabric of who we are.

Doesn't that make you wonder why?

* * *

In a godless universe, I think it's pretty hard to explain, to be honest. I know people try to come up with convincing explanations based on survival and genes, but they usually end up in a terrible muddle, because they have to try to work out why some people beat up their children (who carry their genes) and then give money to charity to help people on the other side of the world (who don't), and why people who have plenty of resources still want more money, and why a guy can get a vasectomy but it doesn't stop him wanting to have sex with everything that moves, and all that. So Freud, Skinner, Maslow and co all have some interesting things to say, but none of them seems to account for the complexities of what it is to be human. They struggle to explain the screaming I heard two nights ago between a mother and daughter who live on my street, and the fact that I desperately wanted to intervene because I had a deep sense that it wasn't right (where did that come from?), and the fact that I didn't.

Suppose for a moment, though, that what I've been saying about the likelihood of a Creator is broadly true. And suppose that this Creator is personal (as somewhere between 3 and 4 billion people on earth believe; I know that doesn't mean they're right, but there's no obvious reason why they couldn't be). If that were the case, then I'd expect the problems with the world, and particularly the problems with humanity, to have something to do with their relationship to that Creator.

If something had gone badly wrong between humans and their Creator, and for some reason a relationship that was supposed to be beautiful had been broken and had gone sour, then I'd expect it to taint everything.

I'd expect the world to be filled with greed (as people tried to replace God in their affections with stuff), and insecurity (because the perfect love that gave them security had gone), and competition (as people tried to define themselves in the absence of God, desperately seeking validation from somewhere), and conflict (as that competition threatened people's security). I'd expect people to cope with the lack of the knowledge of God by searching, in a panic, for experiences that would fill the void, yet always winding up disillusioned because nothing on earth could do the job. I'd imagine they'd look everywhere for a source of love, security and comfort in a turbulent world – food, drink, sex, religion, fame, drugs, influence, family, wealth, whatever – and some would keep going till they dropped, getting more and more of each because they were never satisfied, pursuing fame's phantom unhappily for years, or having sex with one person after another without really knowing why. Some would be more subtle, and look for validation through being more moral than others, reading *The Independent* and starting charities and recycling, hoping that one day their sense of achievement would show that, despite their failed relationships or business ventures, it was all worth it. Others would just resign themselves to an empty existence and use substances, melancholic poetry and angry music to dull the pain. (Or angry poetry and melancholic music.)

On the positive side, in a world like this, no amount of frantic searching would be able to strip them of their abiding, resilient beauty, the creativity, laughter and empathy that come from being made in God's image. But it would always be a beauty scarred, scuppered, soured by the loss of God, like a Titian painting with obscenities scribbled across it, or a lemon drizzle cake with a hornet in the icing.

* * *

A few years ago I was in the Massif Central in France when I came across a collection of essays by the American writer Donald Miller. I found it completely fascinating. Quite a lot of his essays were about exactly what I'm talking about at the moment: what's wrong with the world, and specifically why humans are the way we are. He said a lot of things that made me think, and several that made me laugh out loud, but one thing in particular stood out. It made sense out of the things I had wondered about for years.

He imagined an alien, sent on a mission to earth to investigate human beings. He asked the question: How would an alien describe people? Once it had got over our appearance, and our technology, how would it sum up what makes us do things? And his conclusion was that the alien would say,

> Humans, as a species, are constantly, and in every way, comparing themselves to one another . . . This is the driving influence behind every human's social development, their emotional health and sense of joy, and, sadly, their greatest tragedies. It is as though something that helped them function and live well has gone missing, and they are pining for that missing thing in all sorts of odd methods, none of which are working . . . They are an entirely beautiful people with a terrible problem.

When I read that, something about it struck a chord in my soul. *An entirely beautiful people with a terrible problem.* The alien's analysis, I remember thinking, was spot on: it explained why we played competitive sports, watched reality TV and game shows, climbed career ladders even when promotions didn't lead to happier lives, associated with cool people and dissociated ourselves from uncool people, thought we were better than other people, and cared about celebrities. Donald Miller went on to say that life was like that game when you pretend you're all in a lifeboat, and one of you has to get thrown overboard, and you have to defend your right to stay there. (I was in a debate like that at university, and it's the only time I've ever been sworn at by a Cabinet politician, but that's another story.) He said that our lives were lived out entirely as if we were defending our right to exist in a lifeboat game, as if someone somewhere would decide we were worth our place because we were richer, prettier, cleverer, cooler, more moral, more athletic than someone else. You can see it with teenagers all the time, like those guys who cluster around outside McDonald's in the evenings and aren't allowed to smile because they are too cool for that. But you can see it with adults too, even if it's better disguised. Just listen to people's conversations in a coffee shop one day, or watch some TV, or flick through a random sample of magazines, and you'll see it everywhere. *It is as though something that helped them function and live well has gone missing, and they are pining for that missing thing in all sorts of odd methods, none of which are working.*

* * *

So here's what I've been thinking. If there is a God, then evil is either in the world because he created it that way, or because he gave free agents the ability to make choices, and we made the wrong ones. Given our respective track records – which can be easily compared just by looking at a night sky, and then reading a daily newspaper – I'd be inclined to think that the Creator should get the benefit of the doubt, and that we are more likely to be responsible. Again, I can't prove it, but it just seems more likely.

That makes me think there might be a very good reason why we see sin, death, evil and suffering as problems to be fought, rather than as everyday realities to be shrugged off with a mildly concerned 'uh-oh': maybe it's because the world was never supposed to contain them, and they're there at least partly because of us. Maybe evil is something that resides within each one of us, and shows itself because we are desperately trying to find love and purpose without our Creator. And that makes me ask the unthinkable question: What if we did something, very early on in our history, that spoiled our relationship with the God who created us, and led to all the other evil that we see? What if this explains both sin and death? Sin – as we struggle to cover our naked insecurity with the fig leaves of fame, sex or whatever, trampling on one another in our panicked bid to secure them. Death – as the Creator, who never intended humans to die, made the painful decision that to allow evil creatures to live for ever would permanently mar his creation. In other words, what if the best explanation of evil and death, and our feelings about them, is something like the fall story which the ancient Hebrews told?

It's easy to miss the main point of the fall story, what with the naked people, the fruit and the talking serpent, but the heart of it goes like this. Human beings are in a perfect garden, destined to live for ever, and in relationship with God. But God gives them a choice – the ability to decide whether to obey him, or whether to know good *and* evil – and they choose the latter. Death is the inevitable consequence of this tragic separation from God, and they are exiled from the garden into the rest of the world, where death reigns unchecked. Whether you believe this story or not, it's been circulating for several thousand years, and I think it's a very powerful explanation of evil.

Imagine it had been your decision. You're offered a choice: either you can have a world of endless good, life and abundance, in harmony with your Creator and the whole planet, or you can choose to reject that in favour of knowing both good and evil, light and dark, life and death. The choice, if you will, is happiness versus independence. I can just imagine the first humans, faced with the same options, quoting 'Invictus' to one another as they made their fateful decision, imagining that they were somehow being heroic in their stubborn pride, like everyone who has quoted it since:

> It matters not how strait the gate,
> How charged with punishments the scroll;
> I am the master of my fate,
> I am the captain of my soul.

Or, more recently, 'I did it my way.'

It's weird, this idea that I might prefer independence to happiness. But I discover it's true every time I sulk, every time I wallow in my wounded pride rather than seeking reconciliation, every time I harbour vengeance or unforgiveness, even as it's eating me up from the inside. *I am the master of my fate*, part of me is saying defiantly when that happens; *I am the captain of my soul, and to hell with the consequences*. Better a captain of the *Titanic* than a porter on the *Queen Elizabeth*.

So I think the Hebrew story of the fall, whether you take it literally or figuratively, is a deeply insightful account of what's wrong with the world. Like Solzhenitsyn, it presents evil as a universal human problem; then it links that problem with our desire to be in charge, rather than ruled by the Creator; and then it links together the human and the planet, so that, as with Hiroshima and Chernobyl, the choices and mistakes of human beings have global consequences. It explains why evil is here, and it also explains why we feel like it shouldn't be. It explains the mysterious paradox of humanity, the way we pine for beauty and justice but can't quite attain them, the tragicomic way we are both the world's problem and its potential solution. I know it's an old story, but if there's a God who made people, it's by far the most compelling explanation I've come across for what's wrong with the world.

7.
THE REDEMPTION OF LONDON: WHAT'S THE SOLUTION?

One of the most sung, loved and quoted songs of the twentieth century is 'Imagine' by John Lennon. Numerous polls around the world have declared it one of the best songs of all time (although I find it curious how often music written by English-speaking white guys within living memory is described as the 'best of all time', as if the Aztecs and the Visigoths would undoubtedly agree with us). In 2004, *Rolling Stone* magazine ranked it third in their top 500 songs ever, which is high praise – and it probably should have been even higher, because the top two were Dylan's 'Like a Rolling Stone', and 'Satisfaction' by The Rolling Stones, which makes me think the magazine's own name was not entirely irrelevant here. But clearly there's something about John Lennon's melodic, wistful dream-world that strikes a chord with modern people.

Most of us want to think that, one day, the world will be better. We look around us and see all the things that are wrong, and we imagine a world without those things. Most of us don't write songs about them, but if pushed, I think we all could. Once we've worked out what is wrong with the world, it's a small step to speculate on what the solution might actually be.

For John Lennon, it was a world with no religion, no wars, no national boundaries, no heaven or hell, no private property, and radical equality of possessions, which curiously is almost identical to the vision of Josef Stalin. (The history of the twentieth century suggests that when Lennon sang, 'It isn't hard to do', he might have been slightly overconfident.) For lots of religious people, it's a life of good works, followed by an after-death escape from this messy and corrupt world, into an eternal disembodied heaven/paradise, where there may or may not be virgins, harps and clouds, depending on your religion. For lots of secular people, it's a world where everyone lives in a democracy and has access to free schools and a job in the service sector, unburdened by truth claims (except secular ones), sexual morality or uneducated people. These visions of the future vary dramatically, but they all function the same way: they identify what's wrong with the world, and then imagine what a world without it would be like.

I for one am not satisfied with any of these solutions. My problem with John Lennon's dream-world is partly that it's already been tried and it didn't work, but mostly that it doesn't reckon with the evil inside people. We don't experience pain just because of the broken world around us, but also because of the broken heart within us, which is why John Lennon was incredibly rich and famous, but he was still quite weird, and very sad and angry about things, and he still wrote bitter songs about Paul McCartney, even though the two had made history and made millions together, and he still seems to have given money to the IRA, and he still hurt his wives and his children, and got hurt by them.

I could say similar things about the secular democracy dream-world, which we're trying right now; although it's better than lots of alternatives, it doesn't seem to be stomping out evil that well. Every time an educated, employed, non-religious person does something awful and gets in the papers – hey, every time they go through the pain of divorce, or lose their temper with their children – it's another indication that teaching people stuff and giving them a job doesn't quite fix things. Personally, I doubt you can solve the problem of evil without sorting out the human heart.

In some ways, though, the good-works-followed-by-escape-to-paradise view is even worse. At least the others try to overcome evil, rather than run away from it. But the idea of dying being the solution, rather than a huge part of the problem, seems profoundly lame to me. It's like admitting defeat, and then pretending it's a victory. And I can't believe that the solution to human evil is just doing good things when you can, either. I mean, everybody I know tries to do good things sometimes, but none of them has ever shaken himself free from the tendency to do the wrong things as well. If the problems with the world are really what the theologians call sin and death, then the escape-to-paradise idea, which lots of Muslims and Christians believe, is worse than useless. It's like when I was a kid, and I knew I was losing a game of Monopoly to my little sisters: I would throw the board and the money up in the air in a sulk, abandon the game, and go off to do something else. Either there's a solution to evil and death, or there isn't, but we can't claim to have beaten our enemies if they're still sitting pretty on the sofa, just because we've quit the game and gone off elsewhere.

* * *

It may sound silly, but if there's a Creator God, and a bunch of humans who are clearly flawed, then I'd assume the solution (if there was one) would come from the Creator God, not the flawed people.

If you don't believe in a god of any kind, of course, you have no choice but to hope in the flawed people. If you're an atheist, you've probably got one of two choices: either hoping with John Lennon that human structures will finally remove our desires to do bad things, or resigning yourself to the grim reality that they won't, and making the best of it in the meantime. A century ago, lots of people would have agreed with John Lennon, because it looked like human history was leaping forwards, and we'd soon be able to stop wars, cure diseases and control the weather. These days, the pendulum has swung the other way, and the idea of solving the world's problems is seen as a pipe dream: technology, transport and communication have improved dramatically, but flawed people have simply found ways of using them to increase their power, their wealth, their security, at the expense of others. So if there's no God, then you've either got to be blissfully naïve, or grimly pessimistic, about the odds on the flawed people sorting everything out.

If there is a Creator God, on the other hand, then there may very well be a solution to evil and death. As we've said already, the concept of God includes the idea of being able to do pretty much anything. But I'm fairly confident that if there were a solution, it would be initiated by the Creator God, and not by us. I don't think any regular person is going to stumble across the answer one day, and write a book, and rid the world of evil. (Several nineteenth-century Americans tried this, and that's where most of our major cults come from.) And I don't think we'll gradually improve, over time, until evil and death become things of the past. I just don't have that much confidence in people, or in human progress.

Instead, I think a solution to evil and death would require the Creator God himself to get involved with the flawed people, on his own terms, and resolve everything that's wrong with the world: the fracture between man and God, and all its consequences. In other words, rather than the solution coming from humans finally getting ourselves together, I think it would have to be an act of rescue, by divine initiative. Or, to be more religious about it, it would have to be an act of salvation, by grace. Nothing else would work.

⋆ ⋆ ⋆

Oddly, that idea is pretty much unique to Judeo-Christianity. I mean, lots of people talk about a God or gods, and an afterlife and religious behaviour, but the idea of salvation by grace is found only in the Jewish and Christian Scriptures. This was so surprising to me when I first realized it, and it's still such a strange idea, that it's worth saying again: in most religions, *people don't really talk about being 'saved' or 'rescued' at all*, because there's no concept of the Creator dealing with evil and death, and sorting everything out. Almost all religious people I've come across, including quite a few who claim to be Christian, either believe that things continue in endless cycles, or that all the good guys parachute out to paradise. The idea of the world being redeemed and set right, with human evil finally dealt with and death overcome, doesn't come into it.

In the Jewish scriptures, on the other hand, the idea is everywhere. In the Torah, we read a promise that God will crush the evil one, and bless all the clans of the earth through a descendant of Abraham, whom we later find out will be a king from the tribe of Judah. In the Writings, we hear that this king will establish a global kingdom in which justice and righteousness triumph, the nations of the world are united, peace spreads globally, and the dead are resurrected.

Then, in the Prophets, we hear ancient songs that describe God's rescue of the world in dozens of ways: sins being forgiven and forgotten, people being given new desires to live rightly, the planet flourishing in abundance, death being swallowed up for ever, and the entire earth being renewed. Here's just one example, from a song that is over 2,500 years old:

'For behold, I create new heavens
    and a new earth,
and the former things shall not be remembered
    or come into mind.
But be glad and rejoice for ever
    in that which I create;
for behold, I create Jerusalem to be a joy,
    and her people to be a gladness.
I will rejoice in Jerusalem
    and be glad in my people;
no more shall be heard in it the sound of weeping
    and the cry of distress . . .
They shall build houses and inhabit them;
    they shall plant vineyards and eat their fruit . . .
Before they call I will answer;
    while they are yet speaking I will hear.
The wolf and the lamb shall graze together;
    the lion shall eat straw like the ox,
    and dust shall be the serpent's food.
They shall not hurt or destroy
    in all my holy mountain,'

                    says the LORD.

I think that's quite beautiful, really. In a world where everyone else believed that the world was an evil to be escaped, or an endless cycle to be endured, this funny little group of monotheists stuck stubbornly to their conviction that the true God would destroy death and rescue his creation, and they sang songs about it.

I love that idea. To be honest, I used to find the idea of escaping the world to float off into the clouds somewhere singing hymns for ever a little bit dull. I thought it must be a happy place, because everybody seemed to think it was, but I never worked out how that could be the case. For me, most of the things that make life exciting are incredibly physical, like food and wine, socializing and travelling, snorkelling and skiing, hugging and kissing, so I wouldn't have looked forward to an existence without them. I didn't really want the world to be stripped of physicality. I just wanted that physicality to be healed, so that the bad bits go and the good bits stay, and get even better. No offence, but I wanted the world to be a bit more like Tuscany and a bit less like Croydon. So reading the Jewish prophets, and seeing them talk about a future where the mountains drip wine and the trees clap and the deserts burst with blossoming flowers, and all the while everybody sings for joy and eats outside in the evenings in their gardens, is very beautiful to me. The Hebrews really believed the world would be set free, just like people would be – and they expressed that redemption in incredibly physical terms.

That's not to say it's true, of course. You can't say something as massive as that just by quoting a Jewish poem, and I wouldn't want to either. It's just to say that they were the only people who even *claimed* it was true, the only voice of hope in a bleak religious landscape, and they still are. That means, if I want to believe in redemption for the earth, a victory over death, and a solution to what's wrong with the world, then virtually my only hope is that the God of Israel will make things right.

* * *

I should say at this point: most of this chapter is speculation. If you're the kind of person who likes facts and logical arguments, then you may well be finding it a bit annoying. I know that saying things like, 'I love that idea' and 'I want to believe' don't count as arguments, and I tend to find people who reason that way rather exasperating, like Humpty Dumpty in *Alice Through the Looking Glass*. I know that my desires play a part in my beliefs; everybody's do. But it's no substitute for logic; I realize that.

So at the moment, all I'm trying to do is to imagine what a solution to the world's problems might look like, whether or not there actually is one. Then, later on, I'll ask how we might know if it was true or not, and whether there's any evidence for it.

Just in case you were curious.

★ ★ ★

I was wondering what a solution might look like, so I went to London. It was a strange decision, but I figured that imagining the redemption of the whole world was impossibly vast, and I'd never manage it. Somehow, imagining the redemption of London seemed more achievable. So I got up early, took the train to Victoria, and got the bus as far as Piccadilly Circus.

I've never been one of those people for whom perfection involves nothing man-made. Lots of people these days talk as if a perfect world would have no buildings or vehicles, but I disagree. I mean, I like being in the middle of nowhere as much as the next man, but the world has always seemed slightly incomplete to me without human activity; I've always thought sweeping harbours are more attractive when they have a smattering of yachts in full sail, and that beautiful architecture can enhance almost any vista. So when I think about a world redeemed, I think of it having cities and culture as well as mountains and meadows. I think of it having cities just like London, with galleries, museums, bohemian enclaves, side streets, markets and theatres. It's just that in my dream-world, the evil that currently taints the whole city has been removed.

It starts in the human soul. In the redeemed London, everybody knows that they are loved by their Creator. This might sound very fluffy and religious, but it's the biggest difference between the redeemed London and the regular one. I don't mean that people believe their Creator is real, or that they are doing their best to impress him; I mean they know that no matter what happens, the God of the universe delights in them, sings over them, loves them like I love my children, only more so.

People who don't know this can give their whole lives to the pursuit of an affirmation that never comes – from careers, lovers, children, parents – because we are all wired to get our sense of meaning and security from beyond ourselves. That's why the people going past the window right now are walking so fast, because they're trying to balance their family, their social life and their work, so that their friends, their families or their boss will say, *Well done, you are a worthwhile and meaningful person.* But in the redeemed London, people walk much more slowly, because they already know they're worthwhile and meaningful, because God says so, and he's the only one that matters.

This means that people in the redeemed London live without anything to prove, in complete security, and this has all sorts of implications that make it hard to recognize it as London, even though Tower Bridge and Big Ben and St James's Park are still there. For a start, people on the Tube make eye contact with one another and smile, instead of hiding behind their newspapers, because now strangers are not people to be avoided because they're all scary, but people to be celebrated because they're all happy. There are no brooding clumps of youths standing around Elephant & Castle smoking and looking miserable, trying to find their identity in the acceptance of their group, because all young people in the redeemed London already know who they are and why they matter, since they know and are known by God. The roads are weird: taxis don't cut one another up around Parliament Square or Hyde Park Corner, nobody honks their horn in frustration, bus drivers look happy, and you can't hear any sirens. And because there's no insecurity any more, everybody loves diversity, and you see white people stopping Arab people in the street to ask them about all the beautiful things in their culture, and how to enjoy a really long meal, and how to greet people properly.

People's hearts have changed, too. It's like everybody's got new desires, new passions, because they are all pursuing their happiness in the joy of God and the joy of others, and that changes the way they do everything. *Metro* doesn't have any negative stories any more, and nobody kills or abuses or cheats on anyone. It's not just that people don't do bad things; it's that they don't even want to. There's no hatred in Tower Hamlets, no greed in Kensington, no jealousy in Primrose Hill and no lust in Soho. Beauty is celebrated, but without anyone trying to own it to the exclusion of others. The seedy brothels north of Chinatown stopped operating long ago, not because someone made a law about it, but because nobody wanted to cheapen something as beautiful as sex by having it with a woman they didn't know in an underground hovel. The billboards in Hackney and Southwark, which used to have obscene graffiti over a plea to gunmen to hand in their weapons, now tell stories about how people who used to use graffiti and guns found forgiveness and acceptance and had their lives changed. It's as if the whole city has lost the ache in its soul, the ache people were trying to soothe with money, sex and power. People are living satisfied, fulfilled lives, and it makes the city so beautiful it makes you want to weep.

The oddest thing about the redemption of London is the way people work. In the old London, people would work to get money, as much as they could, so they could get more stuff, look and feel more important, go on nicer holidays and live in nicer flats. In the new one, people still work, but they do it not so much for their own benefit as for the whole community. The City is still there, but all the financial whizz-kids spend their best years trying to work out how to use money to help the most people. All the advertising agencies up by Goodge Street use their creativity and communication skills to praise what is honourable and admirable for its own sake. Oxford Street, would you believe, has become a massive open-air market, where every product you can find is crafted with care, from the exquisite and artistic clothing to the rich selection of handmade books, to the range of fresh breads from the baker who set up where the tacky souvenir vendor used to be. Every square inch of the city has had the good reinforced, and the bad removed, and it spills over into the arts scene, the architecture, the public spaces, even the government. It's a sight to see.

That's something like how I imagine the redemption of London to look, at least in outline. Essentially, it's a city full of people who know they are loved by God, and to whom he has given new desires, so they pursue his purposes instead of their own, and love others as they love themselves. Having said that, I know a city like this is impossible without the Creator God making it happen that way, and I know that without a God, my dream-world is no more achievable than John Lennon's was.

But if there is a Creator, and I think there is, then I'd expect the solution to be about redemption, not abandonment, and fundamentally about the healing of people's souls by restoring their relationship with God, not just the adjustment of the landscape, or the weather. You can have all the lagoons and vineyards you want, but if people are still wandering round with an ache in their souls, desperately searching for something they hope will satisfy them, then we'll just end up polluting the lagoons and turning the vineyards into car parks. In other words, there's no solution for anything without fixing the hole in the human soul. If history tells us anything, it's that it doesn't take more than a few greedy and selfish people to turn the most abundant paradise into chaos. That's what my Zimbabwean friends all say, anyway.

* * *

It's worth saying, though, that if the problems with the world exist because human beings chose independence over happiness, and rebellion against the Creator over submission to him, then redemption would need to include the Creator making us right with him.

That sounds fairly easy, but it isn't. All the monotheistic religions agree that we were created to have an unbroken, exclusive relationship with our Creator, but we decided to take charge ourselves, and we gave ourselves to gods of our own making instead. If that's true, then it isn't trivial. Far from it. It's the ultimate act of betrayal, the equivalent of abandoning your partner, rather than parking on double yellows.

Sometimes people think of 'sin' as a rather petty idea, as if the Creator of the earth shouldn't care what human beings get up to. But I don't see it like that. I think if God made us in his image, for relationship with him, then our running off and worshipping something else would be the biggest slap in the face imaginable. I think a personal God would find it extremely painful.

If you've been cheated on, you'll know that forgiveness isn't easy. In effect, it involves taking upon yourself all the pain and evil the other person committed against you, and absorbing it, soaking it up, so that there is none left to spill out in vengeance or violence. Personal betrayals don't just disappear into the ether. The pain has to be borne by someone – either by the betrayer, or the one betrayed.

I think that's very important to remember if you ever hear talk about the Creator 'taking our sins upon himself', or similar language. I find people are sometimes surprised that God would need to do something like this, wondering why he can't 'just forgive'. But from where I'm standing, the very nature of forgiveness is that you bear the full force of someone else's evil upon yourself, and in doing so find a way to set them free from what they've done to you. So if we were to be made right with our Creator, we would need him to find a way of taking our sins upon himself, and reconciling us to him through it, forgiving us *en masse* for all the things we'd done wrong. We'd be hoping for something like this (from another ancient Jewish song):

> Surely he has borne our griefs
>   and carried our sorrows . . .
> All we like sheep have gone astray;
>   we have turned – every one – to his own way;
> and the LORD has laid on him
>   the iniquity of us all . . .
> by his knowledge shall the righteous one, my servant,
>   make many to be accounted righteous,
>   and he shall bear their iniquities.

The reality is, either God takes our betrayal upon himself, or we carry on floundering in it ourselves, and I know which one sounds more like a solution to me.

* * *

I think we can learn a lot from the ancient songs in the Jewish scriptures. The poets who wrote them were very aware that the problems with the world have an awful lot to do with human evil, so when they talked about a future where everything had been made right, they spoke a lot about it happening through the Creator's initiative, in forgiving and forgetting, renewing and revealing. I think, if there were a Creator God, and if he could pull all that off – if he could forgive our countless mistakes, demonstrate his infinite love and transform our evil desires – then assuming we accepted his gift, I think we'd be very close to having a world without problems.

The final thing to be eradicated, though, would have to be death. A redeemed London, and a world without evil, would be far, far better than the world we're in now, but as long as we still had funerals and cancers and miscarriages, I don't think anyone could say it had been made right. No matter which way you slice it, you cannot have a solution to the world's problems in which death continues to reign, uninterrupted and unchallenged, while we meekly accept the fact and drift off to an ethereal existence in the sky.

I just couldn't hold to a view like that. From my perspective, the Islamic view of paradise, and the popular Christian one of an eternal disembodied heaven, are not so much *answers* to the problems of death as *restatements* of it. No matter how nice people are to one another in the floaty dream-world they talk about, I can't see how you could call it a solution, unless death had been booted out of creation for ever, never to return. Put bluntly, I cannot imagine a solution to the world's problems that doesn't involve resurrection.

★ ★ ★

So here's where I've got to. I think a solution to the world's problems would involve the Creator doing four things: affirming his unconditional love for people, forgiving us for our evil and our betrayal, changing our hearts so that we wanted to love him and love other people, and bringing about resurrection from the dead. Maybe it's not surprising, then, that this is exactly the future the Jewish prophets and poets used to talk about.

It might be a huge pipe dream, of course. That's one of the annoying things about the human psyche – we can want to believe things so much that we can convince ourselves they're true, in the face of all the evidence. Just because we want to believe there's a solution to the world's problems, it doesn't mean there actually *is* one. Just because the Jewish prophets believed in a future world where evil and death had been eradicated, doesn't mean *we* should.

But we have got something to go on. If something like what the Jewish prophets and poets said was true, then we would expect the Creator to have acted in divine grace, taken our sins upon himself, revealed to us his unconditional love, given us his Spirit so our desires changed, and overcome the power of death, as part of the renewal of the whole creation.

So, if it was claimed by over a billion people that the Creator of the universe had done just that – had become human, demonstrated his unconditional love in his life and death, shown us what eternal life was like, died to forgive sins, risen from the dead, given his Spirit to his people, and said he would return to complete creation's renewal – well, that would sound very much like what I'd have expected the solution to be. So I would want to look very carefully into that whole story, and see what evidence there was for any of it.

8.
THE DUBLIN DISPLAY CASE: WHAT HAPPENED ON 9 APRIL AD 30?

The difference between a good city and a great city is the amount of time you can wander around without actually doing anything. In good cities, there are plenty of interesting things to do, but in great cities, you don't really need to do that much, because the most compelling thing about them is just browsing their streets, people-watching and drinking in their atmosphere, getting acquainted with their personality. The genius of New York isn't the Empire State Building or the Statue of Liberty; it's walking across Central Park before the city wakes up, then going south down Madison as far as 42nd Street and arriving just in time to see the suits scurrying about in the morning rush hour with their cellphones and bagels. In Rome, the Colosseum's nice, but pretty much like it looks in the photos; the unmissable experience is the early-morning light in the Centro Storico, as you sit outside Caffè Sant'Eustachio sipping the world's best espresso, watching old men sweep the cobbled streets beneath shuttered windows, and occasionally shouting to one another in Italian words that you can't understand but wish you could.

One of my favourites is Dublin. Rachel and I stayed near Trinity College, so we used to stroll through it on our way towards the city centre, before drifting aimlessly through the maze of little side-roads south of Dame Street, peering down the alleys and weighing up where sold the nicest coffee. Then we would go down to St Stephen's Green and look at the lake and the statues of Oscar Wilde and James Joyce, read for a bit, head north again for lunch at Gruel (which sounds horrible, but sells the best sandwiches you've ever had), meander around the river in the afternoon, then find a quintessential Irish pub – all dark wood, bar stools, half-empty bottles of whiskies you've never heard of, and old boys reading the *Irish Times* – and make our pints of Guinness last as long as possible. We'd get home at the end of the day to discover, to our delight, that we hadn't really done anything.

But one day I sold out, and decided to visit the Chester Beatty Library. You might think that a strange choice in a city with the Trinity College Library and the Book of Kells, but I wanted to see the Chester Beatty Library, which contains a magnificent collection of old documents, including some very early manuscripts of the New Testament. I find something quite enticing about old documents: the fact that they were written before the World Wars, before Shakespeare, before English, while everyone in Britain was drinking the blood of their dead or whatever we used to do; the way they're written in capitals in a foreign language, without any punctuation, on a piece of mashed plant stem. So I raced round the other exhibits, ignoring pretty much everything, until I reached the glass display cases with the second-century New Testament papyri. Then I stopped, and with a block of Greek capitals in front of me, stared in wonder for a long, long time.

Until that point, the most surreal moment of the entire trip had been the pint we had had on the top floor of the Guinness Factory – which, with magnificent oddness, is pint-glass-shaped. How do they get planning permission for these things?

It seems so random that there was a meeting somewhere, and the Guinness executives were asking for permission to build a museum, and the planners said no, because Dublin is one of the world's most expensive and historic cities, and then somebody said, *But of course, if you built it in the shape of a giant pint glass, then your application would sail through*, and everyone else nodded enthusiastically. In most old cities you can't get permission to build a garage, let alone a hundred-foot-high beer glass with a viewing gallery on top.

But the Chester Beatty Library trumped all that. Here I was, looking through a glass display case at a bunch of ancient historical documents, written within a couple of lifetimes of the events they described, which said that a Jewish prophet called Jesus of Nazareth had been raised from the dead on what we have since calculated was possibly 9 April AD 30. They said that this event, which was witnessed by hundreds of people, was the turning point of history, and it meant that the Creator God had taken it upon himself to redeem the earth, forgive people's sins, demonstrate his love and provide a solution to all the world's problems.

If that's true, I reflected, then the world is a totally different sort of place from what people think. It's probably the most important thing that has ever happened.

* * *

So how could we ever know that something like that had actually occurred? We can't do a scientific experiment to test it, and it's not like we can look at satellite footage or anything. Instead, as I talked about in chapter 2, we've got to look at all the available evidence, and work out which explanation fits the facts more coherently and simply than the others.

I guess the best place to start is to summarize the evidence, so here goes. There are at least seventeen documents from the first century that talk about the resurrection of Jesus, written by at least seven different people, and you can go and see very early copies of all of them in glass display cases in Dublin, Cairo, Florence, London, Oxford, Philadelphia and elsewhere. One of the earliest, a letter by a Jewish tentmaker to a church in Greece, is universally recognized to have been written by AD 55, which is only twenty-five years after the resurrection is said to have happened. It says,

> For I delivered to you as of first importance what I also received: that Christ died for our sins in accordance with the Scriptures, that he was buried, that he was raised on the third day in accordance with the Scriptures, and that he appeared to Cephas, then to the twelve. Then he appeared to more than five hundred brothers at one time, most of whom are still alive, though some have fallen asleep. Then he appeared to James, then to all the apostles. Last of all, as to one untimely born, he appeared also to me. For I am the least of the apostles, unworthy to be called an apostle, because I persecuted the church of God.

That's a pretty meaty piece of evidence, and as I say, there are at least sixteen others from the next few decades. But there's more than just what we might call positive evidence. There are no first-century documents that say things like, *Well, lots of people say that Jesus the Messiah was raised from the dead on 9 April AD 30, but they're all discredited these days, because we found his body.* If you assess the evidence purely by the numbers of documents for and against the resurrection happening, then it works out at 17–0.

Of course, we don't do history just by asking for a show of hands. It's just as well, because otherwise seven cranks could get together and write documents claiming the Prime Minister was secretly married to a goat, and if nobody from Downing Street wrote a rebuttal, then the story would stick. (That sort of thing happens quite regularly on election days, I've noticed.) But I think these seventeen documents deserve more consideration than that.

For a start, they're spread across several decades and even countries, and show clear signs of literary independence (that is, they weren't made up by a group of friends in a smoke-filled room somewhere). They're written by a bunch of people who, it is historically certain, did not expect anyone bodily to rise from the dead in the middle of history, so it's not like they made it all up because they hoped it was true. We also know from history that sizeable communities of people, all around the Eastern Mediterranean, accepted the resurrection story as historical fact and reordered their entire worlds as a result, changing their day of worship to Sunday, and often sacrificing their possessions, reputations, families and even their lives because of it. That doesn't mean they were right; people do all sorts of weird things sometimes. But it does mean that the seventeen documents I saw in Dublin were taken seriously by lots of people, and that the absence of any evidence contradicting them is at the very least slightly surprising.

The bottom line is, if we rummage around the first century for evidence about whether the resurrection happened, and if we then find that all the relevant documents say that Jesus of Nazareth, the Jewish artisan-turned-prophet who was executed by the Romans on Friday 7 April AD 30, rose bodily from the dead on the Sunday, then I think we have a responsibility as historians – and, for that matter, as thinking people – to try to find an explanation.

★ ★ ★

So what happened on 9 April AD 30? It's a question I've thought about a lot, and I've come to realize I have only two major options at this point.

The first is to say: nothing in particular. I've come across a surprising number of people who still believe that Jesus of Nazareth didn't even exist, which is such an oddball view that historical scholars don't bother responding to it. (In the words of one academic, it would be like astronomers responding to the view that the moon is made of green cheese.) A number of others agree that Jesus existed, but believe that nothing at all happened on Easter Sunday: the sun rose as normal, a few disillusioned Jews grieved for their dead friend, and that was that. Often, people like this will dismiss all the documents from Dublin by saying that they can't be true because they were later included in the Bible – which, for my money, doesn't quite follow! Alternatively, I remember a guy called Steve emailing me to say that we should only accept evidence from independent witnesses who weren't Christians – but since a Christian is, pretty much by definition, someone who believes in the resurrection, Steve was effectively saying that if people believed in the resurrection, their evidence didn't count, which is a bit of a 'heads-I-win, tails-you-lose' argument. If believing something took place makes your evidence invalid, then how can there be any evidence for anything? So whatever we might say about that Sunday morning, I very much doubt nothing happened.

The second option, which I think makes far more sense, is to draw two conclusions from the evidence: the tomb of Jesus was empty on the morning of Sunday 9 April, and over the next few weeks a number of different people saw appearances of Jesus, which they understood to mean that he had risen from the dead. Personally, I can't see how you can account for the evidence without those two conclusions – the appearances, whatever they were, are just so numerous and so widely witnessed that you can't dismiss them, and the empty tomb is close to being a historical certainty, for the simple reason that it is almost impossible to explain the belief in the resurrection without it. Sooner or later, somebody would have checked to see if the tomb really was empty – bearing in mind it was in Jerusalem, the same city as the Jewish Christians who were preaching the resurrection – and if the body had been there, that would have been the end of it.

That was the conclusion I reached in my early twenties. When I studied the documents in more detail, though, I bumped into a whole bunch of other reasons to confirm it. Imagine, for a moment, that there was no empty tomb and there were no appearances, and many years later, people invented stories like that to support the theological beliefs of their communities. What sort of stories would they have written? I think they would have written stories that backed up their beliefs about what had happened and why it mattered – stories which turned the beliefs of their communities into history.

Yet they didn't. We know from the letter I quoted just now (which we call 1 Corinthians) that by AD 55 people believed three big things about the resurrection of Jesus: it was the fulfilment of the Jewish scriptures, it was witnessed to by a number of leading men in the early Christian movement, and it resulted in personal hope of resurrection for Jesus' followers. But the resurrection stories in the four Gospels are nothing at all like that. They don't link Scripture to the resurrection. The people who find the empty tomb are a bunch of crying women on an early spring morning (which you would never invent if it wasn't true because women in Jewish culture back then were not taken seriously as legal witnesses, so if you were trying to shore up a dodgy story, you'd choose well-known men rather than infamous women). The stories make no mention at all of personal resurrection for Jesus' followers. In short, if the stories had been invented many years later, they wouldn't have looked remotely like they do. To me, that suggests that they weren't invented in the first place.

Funnily enough, as I've read into the subject more and more, I've found that these conclusions are shared by a wide range of historical scholars, from the firmly Christian to the firmly not. I think that's very interesting. When you read books of historical scholarship on this stuff, you don't find many serious academics saying, *What's the big deal? The body was in the tomb all along, nobody saw any appearances of anything, and it was all a big mix-up. Idiots.* Instead, you find people wrestling with these two historical fixed points – the appearances and the empty tomb – and trying to make sense of them, even when they clearly believe that bodily resurrection is impossible. That, for me, is a big hint that these two conclusions are the best way of explaining the evidence.

* * *

For lots of people, I've discovered, even talking about 'evidence' for the resurrection of Jesus seems bizarre.

When I first left university, I became a management consultant in London, and lived in a flat near Highbury Corner with my friends Greg and John. We often used to stay up late, talking about everything and nothing: comedy, microeconomics, literature, whatever. Then, much more recently, we had our first-ever conversation about the resurrection. I'm not sure why, but in all the years I'd known them, it had never come up in conversation. And I noticed, as we talked about it, something quite remarkable: neither of them had ever thought about the resurrection as something for which there might be evidence. To be honest, they were astonished that anybody could even think that way – to them, statements like 'the resurrection happened' were religious statements, not historical ones, and religions operated independently of evidence. It wasn't that they had both looked into it and concluded that the resurrection never happened. It was that they had assumed not only that there wasn't any evidence for it, but that no thinking person even thought there was, so it wasn't an issue worth considering.

I found that surprising. Whatever happened that Sunday morning, it brought into being a group of people numbering upwards of 1 billion (including quite a few thinking people), and its impact has been felt for twenty centuries in almost every country on earth, including ours. Yet some of the brightest and most interested people I know had never really thought about what had happened, and had assumed that it was simply a private religious experience – even though, as I said to them, that didn't begin to make sense of the evidence. I began to wonder how many other people were like that.

* * *

Back to 9 April AD 30: we have an empty tomb, and over the next few weeks a variety of appearances of Jesus, seeming very much alive, to a number of different people, some of whom had followed him before, and some of whom (like Jesus' brother James, and Paul) hadn't. As historians, or just as thinking people, how do we explain that?

I've come across all sorts of theories, and most of them are fairly silly. Some suggest that the women went to the wrong tomb (which sounds very sexist to me), and nobody thought to check whether it really was empty, even when the Jewish authorities were doing their best to stop the Christian movement. Some say the disciples stole Jesus' body and then lied about it, pretending that the resurrection had happened when they knew all along that it hadn't, even though some of them ended up dying for it. Others have claimed that Jesus didn't really die on the cross, and having had his back ripped apart, his feet nailed to a piece of wood and his heart punctured with a spear, he somehow revived in the cool of the tomb, managed to roll aside a stone as heavy as a Volkswagen and overpower two soldiers on his own, and then travel the country for five weeks with neither the ability to walk nor a functioning heart, convincing all and sundry that he'd been resurrected, before disappearing into thin air. It is even suggested sometimes that the authorities stole the body, but were so unthinkably dim that they didn't think to produce it when they were trying to stop people announcing Jesus had risen. The fact that such theories exist at all may just show the gullibility of modern people, but it may also indicate a desperation not to believe in the resurrection, no matter what. I have to admit, I've never taken any of them that seriously.

To my mind, there are only two ways of approaching the question of what happened on 9 April AD 30 that hold any water at all, and virtually every intelligent person I've come across takes one of the two. One is to say that Jesus of Nazareth rose bodily from the dead. The other is to say that, no matter what the evidence might suggest, you can't talk about supernatural events in a historical enquiry like this, so there has to be another explanation. That's pretty much it.

* * *

In Massachusetts, in March 2006, there was a debate between Bart Ehrman and William Lane Craig that sums up these two positions very well. I read the transcript online, and it makes fascinating reading, because the debate isn't really about the historical data (the empty tomb and the appearances), but about whether or not historical evidence for the resurrection could ever be possible. As a Christian, William Lane Craig argued that the resurrection of Jesus was the best historical explanation for the evidence. Bart Ehrman's response, rather than giving an alternative explanation, was to argue that historical evidence of a 'miracle' was by definition impossible, so no matter how unlikely the alternatives seemed – and he didn't really propose any – they must be more likely than a supernatural event. In other words, he wasn't so much saying that there *wasn't* any historical evidence for Jesus' resurrection, as much as he was saying that there *could never* have been. Supernatural events, Bart Ehrman said, can be theological conclusions, but not historical ones.

I thought that was a fairly clever strategy. What Bart Ehrman did that day was to define 'history' in such a way as automatically to exclude all God-things, including the resurrection, from being considered 'historical' – they were now merely 'theological' (which, if I'm not being unfair, basically means 'you can believe them if you like, but if you do, it'll be because of blind faith, not evidence'). At one point, someone asked him if he thought there could ever be historical evidence of a miracle, and to his credit, he admitted he didn't. In other words, Bart Ehrman was saying, it doesn't matter how much evidence you have for the resurrection; I still won't believe it, because history can't involve God doing anything. Or, more bluntly, *I believe there's no such thing as a God who is involved with history, so any accounts of God doing something in history must be wrong, no matter what the evidence.*

The problem with all that, from my perspective, is what I was talking about in the first half of the book, especially chapter 5. You really can't be sure that there isn't a God – actually, there might well be one, for various reasons – and since God could presumably do anything he wanted, you can't be sure that miracles don't happen either. If I were to look at the Dublin display case with an unshakeable conviction that there is no God, then of course I'd have to find another explanation. (If I looked at Elizabethan literature with an unshakeable conviction that there is no Shakespeare, I'd end up in a similar position.) But if I went to the Dublin display case with an open mind about whether God existed or not, I might find that Bart Ehrman's argument wasn't that strong after all.

* * *

Once or twice, I've met people who think like Bart Ehrman. Conversations, if you strip out all the niceties, basically go something like this:

'So tell me: why don't you believe in a God who acts in the world?'

'Because there's no evidence for his existence.'

'What about the resurrection of Jesus?'

'It never happened.'

'There's lots of evidence for it, though, isn't there?'

'Maybe, but there must be another explanation.'

'Why?'

'Because supernatural events don't happen.'

'How can you be so sure?'

'Because a God who acts in the world doesn't exist.'

'Ah.'

And round it goes again. It's like talking to David Hume, on loop.

* * *

That's probably all very unfair of me. I know people don't always say what they mean in live debates, and I also know that you mustn't attack straw men – if you're engaging seriously in discussion about something important, you need to engage with it in its strongest form. I find books that only quote one side of the argument a bit annoying, actually.

So I thought the best way to draw this chapter to some sort of conclusion would be to interact briefly with the two leading scholars to have written books on the resurrection in the last ten years. One of them believes Jesus was bodily raised from the dead by the God of Israel, and one of them believes that, since the resurrection story simply cannot be true, there must be an alternative explanation. They are arguably the two greatest historical Jesus scholars of their time, and there aren't many serious books in the entire field that don't quote either of them: N. T. Wright, Research Professor of New Testament and Early Christianity at the University of St Andrews, and Geza Vermes, Professor Emeritus of Jewish Studies at Oxford.

The two books, which in total comprise a thousand pages, agree on almost everything. They agree on what the word 'resurrection' means – a body coming to life, never to die again. They agree that nobody in the Jewish or Greek worlds expected it to happen to one person in the middle of history. They agree that, as a result of 9 April AD 30 and the weeks just after it, a group of Jewish people began proclaiming that the unthinkable had happened, that the Jewish prophet Jesus of Nazareth had been raised, and that this meant the new creation had started within the midst of the old one. They agree that this is such a dramatic development that it can only be accounted for by the two conclusions I mentioned earlier – the empty tomb, and the appearances or visions of Jesus. They agree that the variety of explanations sometimes proposed for these two facts (a stolen body, the wrong tomb, 'spiritual resurrection' and so on) do not stand up to scrutiny, and in some cases are comically weak. When I read through both books, I was amazed at how similar they were in their analysis.

The only real disagreement comes at the very end of each book, where both writers say what they believe actually happened. For Wright, the empty tomb and the appearances are both sufficient conditions (as in, they would be enough to generate the evidence we have) and necessary conditions (as in, you couldn't get the evidence we have without them) – and the only credible way of accounting for these two facts, he says, is the explanation the first witnesses gave: that Jesus had been resurrected. This leads him to the conclusion that Jesus was indeed raised bodily from the dead on the Sunday:

> Historical argument alone cannot force anyone to believe that Jesus was raised from the dead; but historical argument is remarkably good at clearing away the undergrowth behind which skepticisms of various sorts have been hiding. The proposal that Jesus was bodily raised from the dead possesses unrivalled power to explain the historical data at the heart of Christianity.

He admits that this belief means that you need to rethink the whole world, and even the way you know things, but after a thorough and exhaustive study, he concludes that it is the best explanation available.

For Vermes, on the other hand, 'not even a credulous non-believer is likely to be persuaded by the various reports of the resurrection; they convince only the already converted'. I'm not sure that's true, considering how many people say that they came to Christian faith by investigating the resurrection, but what's interesting is his reason for saying so: 'None of them satisfies the minimum requirements of a legal or scientific enquiry.'

That sentence is practically the only place in the whole book where he explains why he doesn't believe Jesus rose from the dead, and I think it's quite revealing that he says it's for 'legal and scientific' reasons. Legally, he has explained several times, women were not acceptable as witnesses in first-century Judaism, although I doubt many people in Britain today would see that as a reason not to believe them now. And I'm not sure where 'scientific enquiry' came from all of a sudden. I mean, you can't do a scientific experiment on something like this, but I thought that's why we need *historical* enquiry. Isn't it?

Anyway, as a result, Vermes argues, we need to 'fall back on speculation' as to what might have happened, speculation which he limits to three paragraphs in his Epilogue, and which, rather oddly, in no way explains the empty tomb.

In the last paragraph of the main book, just before his Epilogue, he sums up where he is coming from. He has just finished debunking all the normal rival explanations, and concludes:

> All in all, none of the six suggested theories stands up to stringent scrutiny. Does this mean that the traditional resurrection concept, i.e. the miraculous revival in some shape or form of the dead body of Jesus, is doomed to failure in the rational world of today? Or is there another way out of this conundrum that may offer an explanation, if not for the physical resurrection of Jesus, at least for the birth and survival of Christianity?

When I read that, I spluttered into my tea. One of the greatest scholars of our time had just conclusively demonstrated the historical authenticity of the empty tomb, and had just demolished all the alternative explanations. So I was waiting for him either to announce that he believed Jesus had risen, or to propose a new theory which I could wrestle with and consider. Instead, on the basis that the resurrection would be 'doomed to failure in the rational world of today', he unexpectedly and frustratingly gave up altogether on the possibility of explaining 'the physical resurrection of Jesus', and instead gave me three paragraphs in an Epilogue explaining the birth of the early church.

It was so odd, and so out of character, that I sat for a while and tried to fill in the blanks. I couldn't believe that his objection was fundamentally a legal one – just because first-century Jews ignored women's testimony doesn't mean we should, and the fact that the different stories vary in some details shows that they are independent, and if anything, adds to their weight as historical sources.

The only thing I could think of was that it came from his comments about 'the rational world of today' and 'scientific enquiry'. Both phrases suggested, at least to me, that Vermes' main reason for rejecting Jesus' resurrection was nothing to do with a lack of evidence, or with a credible alternative, but was simply a matter of believing that modern science had shown it was impossible. (I'm not sure this is a modern idea, by the way; the ancient world knew as well as we do that dead people stayed dead.) In other words, despite the learned engagement with historical sources, Vermes sounded like he was coming from the same place as Bart Ehrman, and for that matter David Hume. It boils down to this: if, in our modern, scientific, rational age, we can be absolutely certain that God doesn't exist and miracles are impossible, then dead people don't rise, so Jesus didn't either.

Right. But what if we can't?

* * *

So I've come to believe that the historical evidence points strongly to an empty tomb on 9 April AD 30 and a sequence of appearances over the next few weeks. And I can see only two explanations for these facts. If you're certain that there is no God, and/or that he isn't involved in history for any reason, then you'll probably say that Jesus cannot have risen from the dead, even in the absence of any obvious alternative. If you think there is a God, or if you think that there might be, then when you peer into the Dublin display case and follow the evidence where it leads, you may well end up believing in the resurrection. I do, anyway.

9.
REPAINTING GOD: SO WHAT?

The obvious next question is: so what?

This is where things often go pear-shaped. I've met lots of people who jump immediately from 'Jesus was resurrected' to 'Christians are right about everything' and 'the Bible is all literally true', without really thinking about whether one follows on from the other. And I've met even more people who have seen stuff like that, and been so put off by it, and so troubled by people jumping from the resurrection to military invasions or free-market economics or gay-bashing, that they do the reverse: if that's what the resurrection means, then I'm not having any of it, thank you. I wouldn't be surprised if the majority of people in the Western world held one of those two opinions.

So it might be worth saying, before we consider what the resurrection really does mean, that I don't think it means any of those things. It certainly doesn't mean that Christians are right about everything, and it's probably true that many Christians are wrong about all sorts of things, including military invasions, free-market economics and gay-bashing. And anyone who believes the Bible is all literally true can't have read all of it, or they'd have wondered why the woman in the Song of Songs has doves for eyes, goats for hair, fawns for breasts, and so on. (Someone on the internet has made a picture of what she'd look like if it was taken literally; if you get a few minutes to Google it, it's very funny.) The resurrection means quite a few things, but it doesn't mean that.

On the other hand, I don't think we should dismiss the resurrection, either, just because lots of people jump to odd conclusions from it. I wrote a newspaper article recently about Anne Rice, the best-selling author of *The Vampire Chronicles* and latterly of the *Christ the Lord* novels, who had just announced she was quitting Christianity because there were so many 'Christians' who said and did such appalling things. For her, Christianity was tainted by association, and she couldn't live with it any longer. I reckon a lot of people are like that about the resurrection. I can understand why, because some of the things 'Christians' do are truly dreadful – but I also think it's a bit sad to throw the baby out with the bathwater, because it's perfectly possible to believe in the resurrection, yet live in a way that embodies love, compassion and grace. Millions of people do, and I think it's because they understand the resurrection far better than the cranks that Anne Rice has come across.

So: if Jesus was raised from the dead, then so what?

* * *

Sometimes, events take place which are so significant that they make some views of the world look much more likely than others. I was in Brighton a few weeks ago reflecting on this, and an interesting thought occurred to me. It was all about the Berlin Wall.

For a good chunk of the twentieth century, much of the northern hemisphere believed one of two big stories about where history was going. If you lived in the Soviet bloc or in

China, the chances were that your view of history involved increasing progress towards world revolution, and ultimately a global society in which there was no inequality or poverty. If you lived in the capitalist West, your view of history was probably quite different: both democracy and the free market were increasingly spreading, except where oppressive governments existed, and since they were better at creating wealth than the communist system, the Soviet experiment was eventually doomed to failure. Both stories made sense within the worlds where they prevailed. Occasionally, people would jump from one to the other, because they were disillusioned or disenfranchised, but most people stayed within their story and assumed that, in time, their view of the world would be vindicated.

I am just about old enough to remember the Berlin Wall coming down in 1989. I didn't understand its implications at the time; as an eleven-year-old at school, it seemed to involve a lot of footage of foreign people celebrating in the dark, and endless renditions of *The Wall* by Pink Floyd. But with hindsight, it's quite obvious that this event, coming as it did on the heels of a series of other developments in Eastern Europe, made a profound difference in the world – because it made one of the two big stories look much more believable than the other. In effect, at least up to a point, the fall of the Berlin Wall vindicated one story (that the free market and democracy would eventually penetrate Eastern Europe and undermine the Soviet bloc), and made the communist one extremely difficult to believe in any longer. Within fifteen years, young, overpaid, capitalist management consultants like me would be staying in fancy hotels on Friedrichstrasse, crossing Checkpoint Charlie on their way to eat out, and working in Potsdamerplatz helping British companies buy German ones.

It didn't settle the issue for ever, of course. There remained, and remain, communist nations on earth, and a number of thinkers who still believe that Marxist ideology could, if applied more effectively, take over the world. There have also been a large number of very dubious things done in the name of capitalism since then. But you can't rebuild the Berlin Wall, and you can't live as if it had never come down (unless you live in North Korea, and maybe one or two other places). The events of 9 November 1989, and those that immediately preceded and followed it, made one of the big stories look much more believable than the other.

I began to wonder if perhaps the resurrection is like that. There are a number of big stories in the world today. Around a billion people believe that the Creator God has come in person to inaugurate the new creation, forgive the sins of human beings, and redeem the world from evil and death. A few hundred million believe there is no such thing as a God, and ultimately no such thing as redemption. Billions of others think that there is a God (or gods), but he (or they) is not that interested in redeeming the world or forgiving people's sins, either because he can't or because he doesn't want to. You might think that there's no way of adjudicating which is right and which is wrong. But here's the thought that occurred to me in Brighton: *the resurrection of Jesus makes one of these stories look much more believable than the others.*

From where I'm sitting, it's pretty difficult to make the resurrection fit with the view that there's no God, no meaning and no redemption. That's why people like David Hume and Bart Ehrman and Geza Vermes believe it didn't happen – they don't believe that it fits with the view of the world they have. And they're right. It doesn't.

Perhaps surprisingly, it doesn't fit with most religious perspectives either. Given the Hindu or Buddhist view of the world, the crucifixion and resurrection of a monotheistic Jewish prophet would be the last thing you'd expect. Muslims believe that the resurrection is incompatible with Islam, and there are probably other smaller religions that say this sort of thing, too. To be honest, unless you believe in a Creator God who is acting to forgive sins and redeem creation, it's hard to see how the resurrection of Jesus could make any sense at all. (I'll be thinking about how it does make sense later in this chapter.)

I don't think this settles everything. There have been a large number of very dubious things done in the name of Jesus since then, and there are a lot of thinkers who still think that their ideology can, if applied more effectively, take over the world. But you can't undo the resurrection, and I don't think you can live as if it had never happened (unless you live in North Korea, and maybe one or two other places). From where I'm standing, the events of 9 April AD 30, and those that immediately preceded and followed it, made one view of history look much more believable than the others.

That view of history, in outline, goes like this. The problem with the world is roughly what I talked about in chapter 6: that evil and death are in the world, owing to an early decision by humans to rebel against the Creator and run their own show. And the solution is roughly what I talked about in chapter 7: that the Creator became human; demonstrated his unconditional love in his life and death; died to forgive sins; rose from the dead; gave his Spirit to his people; and promised to return to complete creation's renewal.

I know this isn't the only way of incorporating the resurrection into a worldview. You can't prove big stories like this, and there will always be different ways of seeing things. But this is the way that all the earliest witnesses to the resurrection saw the world, and it's been the view of almost everyone who believes that Jesus rose from the dead in the last two millennia. According to the historical sources, it also seems to be the way that Jesus himself explained what he was doing. It may sound obvious, but if a Jewish prophet tells stories about God's redemptive rule coming on earth through him, and about how he will suffer and die before rising again to accomplish it, *and then it actually happens just like he said*, then this lends quite a lot of weight to those stories. That makes me think that, if the resurrection happened, something like this account of reality is likely to be true.

* * *

The earliest answer to the question: 'So what?' came from the people who witnessed the resurrection in the 30s and 40s AD. They tended to say three overlapping things about what the resurrection meant, and they got into big trouble with the authorities for all of them.

First, they said it meant that Jesus was the Messiah (or 'Christ'), the Jewish king they had been waiting for who would bring his rule of justice and peace to the whole earth, and cause the nations to worship Israel's God. Secondly, they said it meant he was the 'Lord', which was the word the Romans used to describe the emperor (and this effectively amounted to the dangerous announcement that the world's true ruler was Jesus, and not Caesar). And most radically, they said it meant that Yahweh, the God of Israel, had actually become a human in Jesus of Nazareth, so that the artisan-turned-prophet from Galilee, who was crucified under Pontius Pilate and who left an empty tomb behind him two days later, was the one through whom the world had been created in the first place.

At the time, the first two of those claims were the ones that made the most waves. Both of them were highly political, and they infuriated just about everybody. The Jews hated the idea that this crucified prophet was their true king, and the Romans often tortured and killed people who thought they could challenge Caesar's authority. As a result, the early Christians spent the first few centuries regularly being persecuted from pillar to post for political troublemaking.

To me, though, the really shocking claim they made was the third one: that the Creator of the world had become human in Jesus. It took me a long time to grasp how bizarre this statement was, because it had become so familiar; but think about it. The early Christians were not just saying that this man was divine in some mysterious way, because of his inspired work of teaching and healing people. They were saying that there was only one God, and that he had revealed himself in this man, so if you wanted to know what God was like, you needed to look at Jesus. They were saying that the universe's Creator was best understood through a human being who loved people and made friends, who ate meals and went to parties, who told jokes and cried when sad things happened, who built community, told stories, hated arrogance, welcomed losers and criminals and children, got betrayed, confronted hypocrites, healed sick people, forgave sins, died on behalf of his enemies, and conquered death.

No other monotheists, either then or today, had ever said anything even remotely like this. They were saying that Jesus was, among other things, repainting God for us. He was showing humans, with all our muddled conceptions of deity, what the true God was really like.

* * *

The uniqueness of that claim is matched only by its impact.

Writing this book has been something of a journey for me, literally as well as metaphorically. I first got the idea of doing something like this in the depths of winter in Atlantic Canada, when someone asked me how I had come to believe what I believed. I sketched out the chapter ideas in the Dordogne valley in France, sitting by a pool in the early evening while the rest of the family drifted around on inflatables, played cards or made dinner. I came face to face with religious fundamentalism in Kano, and saw some of its consequences at Ground Zero in New York, though I also saw some of its secular equivalents on my travels. I met with pastors in eastern Ukraine who had been forced underground by the militant atheists who ran the Soviet Union, and saw the industrial wasteland that their secular utopia had produced. I wandered around the streets of Paris before anyone was awake one autumn morning, and stared up at Notre Dame, remembering how the atheist revolutionaries had worshipped their new world order by naming it the Temple of Reason, and how Madame Roland had marvelled at the crimes committed in the name of the goddess Liberty, right before they chopped her head off. I peered into glass cases in Dublin, read academic tomes on first-century history in Oxford and Cambridge, reflected on what was wrong with the world in Zimbabwe, and daydreamed about what a redeemed earth might look like in Samoa, Tuscany and New Zealand. And in between times, I sat in coffee shops in Brighton and London, and wondered aloud about truth, origins and redemption.

Wherever I went, though, I couldn't get away from the impact of Jesus. I discovered it was very difficult to find places on earth where he was irrelevant. Wherever I travelled, there were people who had heard of him, people who laughed at him, people who loved him, people who wanted to destroy anyone who followed him, people who swore by him, people who built exquisite buildings in which to worship him, people who said he was alive, and (pretty much everywhere) people who divided human history into the bits before and after him. It seemed strange that this man, who wrote nothing down, rejected violence and had just 120 disciples when he died – disciples who, for the first several centuries, were widely regarded as blasphemous, politically subversive oddballs – should have had such a global impact. Especially when you consider he told people that, if they wanted to be his followers, they had to give up their rights to money, sex, power, idol-worship and everything else they had. It doesn't sound like a winning sales pitch to me.

Yet Jesus was successful in repainting God. He completely changed theology. I mean, you can travel to pretty much any country on earth, and you'll find people there who use the word 'God' in the singular, to refer to a being who is loving, a kind of father, someone to whom people pray in expectation of an answer, who cares about creation and wants to fix it, who is high and exalted and yet can be known by human beings. You even find this use of the word 'God' shared by people who don't believe in one. And it's highly unlikely that, without Jesus, anybody other than Jewish people would think the word 'God' meant anything like that. Were it not for Jesus, we might all still be worshipping the gods of the sun and the moon, dancing around phallic symbols and offering sacrifices, like those disturbing islanders from *The Wicker Man*.

* * *

So let's do some theology for a moment. If the Creator of the universe was revealed in Jesus, what would that show me about God?

It would show me God cared enough about people to become a person, in order to rescue us from ourselves. If I was God, I don't think I'd do that. In the Hebrew story, God is the victim of a shocking act of betrayal, of spiritual adultery, by human beings. But in my experience, if someone abandons and betrays a person who loves them very deeply, and shows no signs of being sorry about it, we don't expect the jilted person to take responsibility for fixing it. And we certainly don't expect them to make massive sacrifices to restore a relationship with someone who rejected them – massive sacrifices like becoming one of them, and being scorned and abused by them, and carrying the weight of all the wrong things they ever did (because somebody has to), and then dying a horrible death in their place. The only thing we'd be able to say of behaviour like that is that it reflected a level of sacrificial love we don't see very often. It would be the kind of love that deserved every poem, every choir and violin, every fresco and canvas that the artists of this world could muster.

It would show me that God was passionate. I know you wouldn't guess this from the stained-glass windows, which make me imagine him as a misty-eyed shaman or an unexcitable religious studies teacher, but the historical records describe a Jesus who lived life in full colour: a man who cried, laughed, shouted, bantered, dozed off, got angry, cracked jokes, knew pain, confronted hypocrisy, put himself in harm's way and told storms to shut up. Not that this has anything to do with it, but I want God to be like that. I think a God who was indifferent to injustice, or whose heart rate stayed the same no matter what was happening, would be far too drab, grey and half-baked to be worth any attention. Say what you like about Jesus, and many do, but he wasn't half-baked.

It would show me that God was unreservedly committed to redeeming the world, but that it would happen gradually. Jesus told stories about this all the time – God's kingdom, he said, is like a mustard seed that you don't notice initially, but becomes a massive tree; like a tiny bit of yeast hidden in a lump of dough that eventually transforms the whole loaf; like a field where good crops and bad crops grow together until the harvest. The empire of God, he was saying, will come quietly, gradually, with bad living alongside good for a while. This bothers lots of us, because we think that a loving God should instantly destroy all the world's problems. But what we often don't notice is that destroying all the world's problems would also mean destroying *us*, because otherwise the rebellion and selfishness in our own lives would continue for ever, corroding creation like an acid. We figure that the kingdom of God, if it exists, should be like Hiroshima: a bomb dropped from the skies that instantaneously obliterates all malice and suffering, and remakes the world in a flash.

But on reflection, I'm glad it's more like Normandy – a bridgehead of God's world established in the middle of ours, with victory assured, but with time allowed for the enemy, which includes me, to embrace God's empire and abandon mine. I know that means waiting a while for the final fall of Berlin, and living in the overlap of the ages with all the pain and frustration that involves, but I can't help feeling it's the most compassionate thing that a God who cares about people could possibly do.

It would show me that God didn't see people the same way we do. We tend to think highly of people who are rich, powerful, intelligent, beautiful, confident, famous; Jesus spent almost all his time hanging out with poor, oppressed, marginalized, hurting nobodies. This is the thing Friedrich Nietzsche hated about Jesus, but it's the thing I love about him. I love this subversive God and his upside-down empire of outcasts, prostitutes, slaves and lepers, where even the twelve disciples were made up of sceptics and terrorists and tax cheats and northern boaties who smelled of fish. I love the idea that the universe is run by someone who sees through our insecure power plays and celebrity culture, and who knows that, underneath the razzamatazz and social hierarchy, we're all broken and we all need healing just the same, and who offers hope and redemption to the odd, the ordinary and the obscure. It's profound, and very beautiful, that God offers rescue to everyone, and that the only people who don't receive it are the people who don't think they need it. You can't say fairer than that.

It would show me all sorts of other things, and this isn't the place to go into them in detail – that's what theology books are for. But when I started wondering about truth, origins and redemption, I grew to love the idea that God, the maker of all worlds who simply spoke and it was so, had expressed himself as a human being who looked, lived and loved something like this. It gave me hope. It made me think that I would probably enjoy spending time with a God like this, and that he would probably enjoy spending time with me, and that if I asked him to forgive me and give me his resurrection life, he'd probably jump at the chance.

*　*　*

Logic can take you a long way. It can get you to accept that evidence is important, that there is a world, and that knowledge is possible (chapters 1 and 2 of this book). It can debunk some of the muddy arguments that lead people to say that the existence of God can be ruled out by science, and can highlight a number of scientific observations that make belief in God just as credible, if not more so, than the alternatives (chapters 3 and 4). Again, reason can take you from here to the realization that the activity of God in the world is not impossible (chapter 5), which in turn casts doubt on the main reason, or perhaps the only reason, that many people reject the very strong historical evidence for Jesus' resurrection (chapter 8). And thoughtful reflection on the world around us can suggest that what's wrong with the world is evil and death (chapter 6), and that any solution would probably involve the Creator, assuming there was one, displaying his love, forgiving sins, changing our desires and conquering death (chapter 7). It can even muse on the implications of all this for our understanding of God (chapter 9).

But that's where reason stops. At least, it did for me. Working things through logically got me so far, but it couldn't prove the existence of God, far less the deity of Jesus or the promise of redemption. It couldn't guarantee that giving up everything to follow Jesus would work. This bothered me, and it still bothers lots of people I know. It wasn't until I started to think about God as a person, rather than a thing, that I was able to resolve it.

Logic works when you're going out with someone. You observe the other person, you think about them carefully, you make predictions about the way they'll behave – sometimes you're right, sometimes horrendously wrong – but you learn, and you begin to form a coherent picture of what married life with them might look like. But because they're personal, not mechanical, you can never be certain how things will pan out until you commit yourself to them. There comes a moment when you have to trust them, surrender yourself to them completely, die to the old you, and embrace the thrilling new reality of being united with someone else. Only once you've done this, and given up everything to be joined to them permanently, can you know for certain that it works. People who aren't prepared to take that step of trust (you could call it a 'leap of faith', I guess, but that always sounds a bit *Indiana Jones* to me) – people like this will never know the joys of marriage, the ecstasy and exhilaration of a love unrestrained. They may hear about it from others, but they will never experience it for themselves, without putting their confidence in another person, surrendering themselves and all they have, and committing to love them and remain one with them for ever.

★ ★ ★

I came to see that this was what Jesus meant when he talked about repenting, and believing, and dying to my old life, and burying it in baptism. In a sense, this all sounded like a high price to pay for the love of my Creator, and in a sense it was. But in another sense, it was simply a description of what responding appropriately to the love of my Creator looked like.

For a long time, I had thought that Jesus was just piling up things I had to do in order to get accepted by God. But I don't think that any more. I now realize he was telling me that love for God, like marriage, involved me leaving the old life behind, trusting the other person completely, holding nothing back, taking on a new identity, and giving up everything for the sake of the only one who mattered.

So that's what I did. You?

discover more great Christian books
at www.ivpbooks.com

Full details of all the books from Inter-Varsity Press – including reader reviews, author information, videos and free downloads – are available on our website at **www.ivpbooks.com**.

IVP publishes a wide range of books on various subjects including:

Biography

Christian Living

Bible Studies

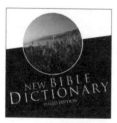
Reference

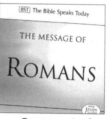
Commentaries

Theology

On the website you can also sign up for regular email newsletters, tell others what you think about books you have read by posting reviews, and locate your nearest Christian bookshop using the *Find a Store* feature.

IVP publishes Christian books that are **true to the Bible** and that **communicate the gospel, develop discipleship** and **strengthen the church** for its mission in the world.